CONTENTS

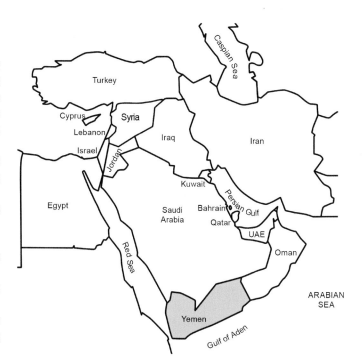

Helion & Company Limited

Unit 8 Amherst Business Centre, Budbrooke Road, Warwick CV34 5WE, England

Tel. 01926 499 619

Email: info@helion.co.uk   Website: www.helion.co.uk   Twitter: @helionbooks   Visit our blog http://blog.helion.co.uk/

Published by Helion & Company 2021, based on material partially published in a different format in 1999 and 2011

Designed and typeset by Farr out Publications, Wokingham, Berkshire

Cover designed by Paul Hewitt, Battlefield Design (www.battlefield-design.co.uk)

Text © David Birtles, Cliff Lord and Tom Cooper 2021

Photographs © as individually credited

Colour profiles © David Birtles, Renato Dalmaso, David Bocquelet and Tom Cooper 2021

Maps © Cliff Lord and Tom Cooper 2021

Cover Photo: Ataq Airstrip, with FNG officers and men in the foreground, ca 1961. Note the sergeant
wearing green overalls and a cotton bandoleer around his waist. (Jim Ellis)

Cover Artwork: No. 8 Squadron, RAF, was one of the units equipped with Hawker Hunter FGA.Mk 9 fighter-bombers, deployed at RAF Khormaksar
in the 1960s. The principal armament of No. 8 Squadron's Hunters consisted of four internal ADEN 30mm guns and unguided 127mm rockets,
up to 24 of which could be installed under the wings (in form of four 'banks' of three rockets under each wing). (Artwork by Tom Cooper)

ISBN 978-1-912866-42-7

British Library Cataloguing-in-Publication Data.

A catalogue record for this book is available from the British Library.

For details of other military history titles published by Helion & Company Limited contact the above address, or visit our
website: http://www.helion.co.uk. We always welcome receiving book proposals from prospective authors.

GLOSSARY OF TERMS AND ABBREVIATIONS

ADC	Aide de Camp
APL	Aden Protectorate Levies
EAP	Eastern Aden Protectorate
FLOSY	Front for Liberation of South Yemen
FNG	Federal National Guard
FRA	Federal Regular Army
GOC	General Officer Commanding
GG	Government Guards
HBL	Hadhrami Bedouin Legion
HKSRA	Hong Kong Singapore Royal Artillery
KAC	Kathiri Armed Constabulary
LTF	Lahej Trained Forces
MARA	Military Assistant to the Resident Adviser
MEC	Middle East Command
MELF	Middle East Land Force
MRA	Mukalla Regular Army
NLF	National Liberation Front
QAC	Qu'aiti Armed Constabulary
QSG	Qu'aiti Sultanic Guard
RA	Royal Artillery
RAF	Royal Air Force
RE	Royal Engineers
RFC	Royal Flying Corps
RGA	Royal Garrison Artillery
RHA	Royal Horse Artillery
SAA	South Arabian Army
SAP	South Arabian Police
STRE	Specialist Team Royal Engineers
WAP	Western Aden Protectorate
WTG	Wahidi Tribal Guard

Lt Col F Robinson, CBE DSO and Commander Aden Protectorate Levies 1928-1939. Robinson was the father of the APL and subsequently of the FRA and SAA. (Frank Edwards)

Lt Col M C Lake, CMG, 4th Grenadiers, Indian Army, who Commanded the 1st Yemen Infantry. (Frank Edwards)

ACKNOWLEDGEMENTS

The authors are very grateful for the assistance given by H.H. Sultan Ghalib of Qu'aiti. Not only did he provide many photographs but he gave much advice and enthusiasm for the project. And in particular he provided considerable detailed information on the Eastern Aden Protectorate and its military forces. H.H. Sultan Ali Abdul-Karim Al-Abdali provided insightful knowledge about the Lahej Trained Forces. Captain Jim Ellis, OBE, the last Resident Adviser in the Eastern Aden Protectorate, provided a detailed analysis of all the military forces in the Eastern Aden Protectorate and huge support for the book. Major General J.D. Lunt, CBE, provided an overview of the military forces of Aden during his time, and Brigadier J.H. Mallard wrote about his Federal National Guard. Maj. Charles R. Butt kept in contact for many years sending both photographs and information regarding his APL days. An Aden Police perspective was provided by F.W. (Dicky) Bird, MBE, GM. Continued support from Tom Wylie, with his photographs and keen interest, kept the authors on track. Dr. Huub Driessen, and Sqn. Ldr. Rana Chhina IAF (Retd.) provided historical research from London and New Delhi. The maps were prepared by cartographer Frank Bailey of Waikato University, and the rank illustrations were drawn by Malcolm Thomas. The information about Arabian Medals and Awards were provided by H.H. Sultan Ghalib and Owain Raw-Rees, an expert in this field. Of special mention is Glen Hodgins for research in India, and Aaron Fox who provided information on weapons, advice and support in many different areas. Shamus O.D. Wade of the Commonwealth Forces History Trust provided much new information. Sean Brady provided many Aden photographs from his collection. Even with their assistance, the authors still owe a great debt of gratitude to many other people and organisations for their assistance, information and help. Many served in Aden and the Protectorates, and have written giving details of their service, and provided historical and uniform details of their units. Without their contributions this book would never have been written. They are: AHB 5 (RAF), Room 411, Ministry of Defence, London; B. Bailey; Raymond Butler; C. Carter; C.C. Carruthers; J.B. Claro, MOD Naval Historical Branch, London; A Clay; Peter Cooke; Bill Cranston; Michael Crouch; R.H. Daly; Alan D'Arcy; Stephen Day; John Daymond; DCLI Museum, Bodmin; Defence Equipment Administration, Crown Agents, Sutton; Department of Photographs, Imperial War Museum, London; Departmental Record Officer (Archives), Ministry of Defence, London; Deputy Keeper, Department of Printed Books, Imperial War Museum, London; Directorate of Public Relations (Army), Ministry of Defence, London; M. Docherty; James Dunn; Wing Commander E.I. Elliott; P.J.V. Elliott, Keeper of Research and Information Services, Royal Air Force Museum, Honington; Fa'iz Fattah; S. Folkes, Reader Services, The British Library, Oriental and India Office Collections, London; W.A. Ford; R.A. Hale; J. Bryant Haigh; D. Hardacre; J.G.R. Harding; M. Harding, Department of Archives, Photographs, Film and Sound, National Army Museum, London; E. Haynes; Royal Artillery Historical Trust, Woolwich; Peter Herrett; Peter Hinchcliffe; Colin Hodgkins, S.K. Hopkins, Department of Uniform, National Army Museum, London; Edward Horne BEM; R.W. Howes, Official Publications Library, The British Library, London; K.G.F. Irwin; A.H. Lawes, Search Department, Public Record Office, D. Leveque, British Library; Kew; I.S. Lockhart, Records Branch, Foreign and Commonwealth

Office, London; J. Longworth, Army Historical Branch, Ministry of Defence, London; Anthony N. McClenaghan; Michael McKeown; Steve Marriott, Police Insignia Collectors Association of Great Britain; Oliver Miles; Todd Mills; Ashok Nath; P. Nuttall; Photographic Section, Public Record Office, Kew; RHQ PWRR, Canterbury; A.H.H. Richardson, Library and Records Department, Foreign and Commonwealth Office, London; Royal Engineers Museum, Chatham; Royal Hampshire Regiment Museum, Winchester; Royal Signals Museum, Blandford Forum; David A. Ryan; W. Stroud, Librarian, *Soldier*, The British Army Magazine; Frank Stevens; A. Thomas, AHB (RAF), Room 308, Ministry of Defence, London; Major General 'Sandy' Thomas CB, DSO, MC; Rex Trye; C. Turner; Peter Waring; Dr Nigel W.M. Warwick, RAF Regiment Historian; Graham Watson; Neville West.

PHOTOGRAPHS

The authors wish to thank the many people who loaned their photographs so they could be included in this book. Special thanks go to the Royal Signals, and *Soldier Magazine* for permission to use their photographs, and David Belson, Crown Copyright Administrator, Ministry of Defence, London for his assistance, H.H. Sultan Ghalib of Qu'aiti for access to his photograph collection, Peter Herrett for his support and photos, and the Tony Ford who provided a superb collection of coloured photographs of the FRA and SAA. Also special thanks go to Sean Brady for sharing his father's collection of Aden photographs.

AUTHORS' NOTE

For those that served in Aden with locally raised forces it is always disappointing to find that their unit rarely gets a mention in any publication. The authors have tried to rectify this by offering a perspective that focuses on the locally raised units that were a permanent feature of the armed forces of Aden. Both Indian Army and British Army units were raised in Aden, and these are also included; however they are not described in as much detail. A general overview of the many regiments that served in Aden during times of crisis is included in the appendices. While writing this book it quickly became evident that South Arabian place names lacked a standardised spelling. Over the years a village may have many different spellings of its name on maps and in books. The authors hope the reader will indulge them by accepting the spelling provided.

This revised third edition has been published due to the demand for more copies and has been placed into the Middle East@War series format which links up with the Gulf States and Oman volumes. More information on the RAF and RN contribution is included. Many new photographs have been added from Sean Brady's collection. Jonathan Paynter's portraits of the many locally raised forces is included, which faithfully depicts the uniforms, flashes, leather equipment and *pagri*.

FOREWORD

CAPTAIN J.N. ELLIS, OBE, DSM (QU'AITI)
Resident Adviser, Eastern Aden Protectorate 1965–1967

Because of its strategic position, Aden has a long and momentous history as an international port, having a magnificent natural harbour at the junction of the Red Sea and the Indian Ocean, but its earlier masters probably had no standardised military insignia as we understand such things and do not appear to have left any

examples. This book is therefore confined to the British era between 1839 and 1967. During this relatively short period a lot happened and many changes took place. In January 1839, Aden was occupied by a force commanded by Captain S.B. Haines of the Indian Marine, the East India Company's Navy. The infantry element of this force consisted mainly of the 26 Bombay Native Infantry who were a Marine Battalion of the 'Honourable Company'. (About half its personnel were 'up-country' types – Afghan tribesmen whose descendants fought on both sides in the recent civil war which tore Afghanistan apart). The unit appears to have remained in Aden for the next six years and still survives in the Pakistan Army today as 7 Battalion of the Baloch Regiment, having served under various names in many wars, large and small, in Persia (several times), Mesopotamia (now Iraq), Afghanistan, Abyssinia, Burma, China, Malta, East Africa and France, where they gained the first Indian Army Victoria Cross. The same unit was back in Aden in the latter part of the First World War as 126 Baluchis. After the Indian Mutiny of 1857, the administrative functions of the East India Company were taken over by the Government of India and its military formations became the Indian Army. Aden was administered until 1937 as part of Bombay Presidency, the western 'province' of India, after which it became a Crown Colony with an adjacent Protectorate. Indian Army units formed part of the Garrison until the end of the Second World War, the soldier's wives earning pin-money sorting the coffee beans for export to Europe and America. In the meantime, Arab military, paramilitary and police forces developed in increasing size and numbers as the Colony developed and these provide most of the material for this book. The authors both served with Arab troops in and around Aden in the 1960s and have taken upon themselves the considerable task of researching and collating the material, a work which no one else appears to have attempted in detail. Indeed, they have provided us with a work of historical as well as specialist value.

Jim Ellis
27 April 1999

PREFACE FOR THE REVISED SECOND EDITION

H.H. SULTAN GHALIB OF QU'AITI STATE IN THE HADHRAMAUT

I deem it a rare pleasure and an undeserved honour to be invited to write the preface to this book, particularly as I have some idea about how much time and effort had gone into assembling and sifting the relevant material for it, before presenting it in the direct and clear language of soldiers. Given the prevailing circumstances, the two authors have left no possible source unapproached or untapped regardless of the difficulties involved and they deserve special credit for their application, persistence and patience.

In brief, this is a unique and accurate history which focuses on the assemblage of information of unquestionable authenticity of a particular nature and concerning a highly important aspect in the region's history during a phase, when it had been drawn into the vortex of international history, so to remain for some 13 decades (between the years 1839 and 1968), starting with Britain's entry onto the scene with the occupation of Aden. What adds further to this contribution is that so little has been written about this region and this era, or for that matter, any era, let alone the highly specialised subject covered by this book.

Being drawn towards the region primarily for reasons of strategic necessity but no direct or immediate economic attractions, Britain since its occupation of Aden was compelled in order to keep its Great Power rivals out of it was to enter into a network of treaties and engagements with its rulers and chiefs offering them recognition, the guarantee of protection from external (and often internal) threats, the favour of friendly advice if sought and some regular financial compense in return for the commitment on their part and that of their heirs to withhold themselves from all contacts and dealings with external powers and entities, as well as to refrain from lending, leasing, mortgaging or selling any part of their territories or possessions without its knowledge and concurrence.

With the passage of time, the spirit of these engagements, at least on Britain's part, was to lead it to greater or more direct involvement in the security and day to day administration of the region as well in support of these rulers tied to it by treaty. This book relates in particular to the machinery that Britain was to help create, or develop and reform, in order to be enabled to manage its treaty obligations towards these chiefs effectively, yet parsimoniously. In this regard, Britain's civil and military representatives in the region undoubtedly deserve great credit for their achievement in maintaining peace and control, almost consistently with a few hiccups in a region and an environment that could easily be described as one of the most difficult and volatile in geographical and political terms to their great credit for nearly 13 decades.

The two authors have definitely saved for posterity and just in time, what was certainly fated otherwise for perdition and eternal loss and have placed before for those interested in the region's history in particular and the world at large, in print, the incredible story of the tools with which Britain succeeded in managing its interests and treaty obligations in this little known and oft ignored by geo-politically important regions of the world during this phase.

The book can also certainly be described as a 'straight from the heart' recognition tribute to the memory and achievements throughout this period of every particle, every single indigenous component or participant member of this military and security system and network on whom the responsibility of seeing to the success of this British mission of maintaining local security fell in actuality and with what dedication, courage, cheer and efficiency they always played their role to the hilt within the parameters of the moral, social and cultural environment and its values as known to them and recognised by them regardless of the odds.

It is also by its very authorship an emphatic statement, even if indirect, on the camaraderie and sincere bonds of friendship, sympathy and mutual respect and understanding that evolve across ethnic, social, cultural and religious barriers between men sharing the same experiences and trials shoulder to shoulder and producing the effort required by the challenges in order to overcome them. In short, the book is one 'in the eye' for those who blindly decry in their entirety the emotional relationships which emerge out of such associations, even if they be between the 'coloniser' and the 'colonised'.

The late David Birtles and Cliff Lord in this instance have left little unturned in their tribute to this relationship and the recognition of the role played by Britain's indigenous partners in assisting it in the conduct of its obligations as a Great Power

by actually carrying the onus of its burden during the period in question.

The deserved by right gratitude of each son and daughter of the region 'till kingdom come' for assembling and saving for posterity all those little known pieces of information of a specific professional military relevance relating to their history and that of their forbearers – the men, the units, their establishment, organisation, purpose, functions, duties, training, dress (ceremonial and otherwise), equipment, transport and all) from the borders of the Yemen of the Imams in the west to those beyond the Rub'al Khali in the North and Oman in the East.

As a son of the region, I feel humbled by the generosity of their effort and contribution as by the genuine nature of their sincere affection for it and its people, sans any strain of bitterness or rancour on any ground whatsoever.

I sincerely offer to them on my behalf and that of my fellow countrymen, our lasting appreciation, gratitude and reciprocated thoughts and good wishes, the finest of them, aye,

Sultan Ghalib bin Awadh al- Qu'aiti
15 May 2010

INTRODUCTION

When Britain left South Arabia in 1967 it marked the end of an era. It was more than just losing another country to independence – it finalised the end of frontier-style soldiering. Although a part of the Arabian Peninsula, there were many links with India. Aden and the Protectorate had been administered by the Bombay Presidency in India until 1937 when it became a colony under the control of the Colonial Office in London.

In the nineteenth century the port of Aden became famous because of its strategic value at the southern-most point of the Red Sea. It was used as a major refuelling station by naval and merchant shipping prior to their departure across the Indian Ocean or journey north to the Suez Canal. Britain had seized the sleepy Arabian town of Aden in 1839 to protect its vital interests in the area, and signed treaties with the various sheikhs and sultans who laid claim to the adjacent coastal lands. These areas were to become known as the Protectorate, later being divided into the Eastern and Western Aden Protectorates (EAP and WAP respectively) for administrative purposes. Each State had its own local military forces for protection, while Britain provided advice and external security. The Protectorate was a collection of States in which emirs, sultans and sheikhs ruled their subjects with absolute authority. *Felix* Arabia was a place where time had stood still for centuries. Peaceful Arabia it had been, but that was destined to change.

The wind of change sweeping through Africa in the late 1950s also blew across the Gulf of Aden to the Colony and Protectorate. There was little that could be done to prevent the onward march of Arab nationalism. Politicians in Britain deemed it necessary to bring all the individual States of the Protectorate into a single federation. In 1959 six of the States in the Western Aden Protectorate united as the Federation of the Amirates of the South, a name that was changed to the Federation of South Arabia when Aden Colony joined in 1963. Most of the States in the Western Aden Protectorate eventually joined the Federation, as well as Wahidi state from the Eastern Aden Protectorate. With the advent of federation, the political situation in the country deteriorated. Opposition came from the South Arabian League, National Liberation Front and the Front for the Liberation of South Yemen.

In 1966 the British announced that their troops would withdraw by 31 December 1968, a statement which immediately triggered a power struggle between the rival factions. Attacks on Government forces increased. Loyalties were reviewed by one and all, and the collapse of the Federation became inevitable. The partially-realised hope of a united South Arabia was shattered by a tortuous civil war, which brought the fledgling Federation and the States of the Eastern Aden Protectorate into one country – The People's Republic of South Yemen.

TREATIES OF PROTECTION

Formal treaties of protection in what was to become the Aden Protectorate started with the Mahra Sultanate of Qishn and Socotra in 1886. Britain initiated a gradual formalisation of protection arrangements that included over 30 major treaties of protection with the last signed in 1954. These treaties, with other minor agreements, created the Aden Protectorate except for the port and immediate environs of colonial Aden which was the only area under full British sovereignty and with some offshore islands, was originally known as Aden Settlement (1839–1932), Aden Province (1932–1937), Aden Colony (1937–1963) and finally State of Aden in the Federation of South Arabia (1963–1967). For British protection, the rulers of the constituent territories of the Protectorate agreed not to enter into treaties with or cede territory to any other foreign power. In 1917, the Government of India, recognising its inability to provide sufficient forces to defend Aden against invading Turkish forces, transferred military control of the Settlement to the War Office and control of the Aden Protectorate affairs to the Foreign Office. For administrative purposes, the Protectorate was informally divided into the Eastern Protectorate with a British Resident Advisor, stationed at Mukalla in Qu'aiti from 1937 to 1967 and the Western Protectorate, which had its own Political Officer in Lahej from 1937 to 1967).

ADVISORY TREATIES

In 1938, Britain signed an advisory treaty with the Qu'aiti Sultan in the East Aden Protectorate and from then onwards until 1954 similar treaties were signed with a dozen other Protectorate States. These agreements provided British Political Officers within some of the States. The States shown in Table 1 had advisory treaties with Britain:

Table 1: States with Advisory Treaties with Britain

Name of State	Protectorate
Katheri	EAP
Qu'aiti	EAP
Mahra	EAP
Wahidi Balhaf	EAP
Audhali	WAP
Beihan	WAP
Dhala	WAP
Fadhli	WAP
Haushabi	WAP
Lahej	WAP
Lower Aulaqi	WAP
Lower Yafa	WAP
Upper Aulaqi	WAP

Table 2: The States of the Federation of South Arabia in 1967

Name of State	Type of State	Date	Province
Alawi	Sheikhdom	1965	WAP
Aqrabi	Sheikhdom	1960	WAP
Audhali	Sultanate	1959	WAP
Aulaqi, Upper	Sultanate	1965	WAP
Aulaqi, Upper	Sheikhdom	1959	WAP
Aulaqi, Lower	Sultanate	1960	WAP
Beihan	Emirate	1959	WAP
Dathina	State	1960	WAP
Dhala	Emirate	1959	WAP
Fadhli	Sultanate	1959	WAP
Haushabi	Sultanate	1963	WAP
Lahej	Sultanate	1959	WAP
Muflahi	Sheikhdom	1965	WAP
Sha'ib	Sheikhdom	1963	WAP
Wahidi	Sultanate	1962	WAP
Yafa, Upper	Sultanate	Never Joined	WAP
Yafa, Lower	Sultanate	1959	WAP
Kathiri	Sultanate	Never Joined	EAP
Mahra	Sultanate	Never Joined	EAP
Qu'aiti	Sultanate	Never Joined	EAP
Aden	Colony	1963	Colony

1

EVOLUTION OF THE MILITARY AND POLITICAL FORCES IN ADEN

THE ANNEXATION OF ADEN

Communication between Britain and India was exceedingly slow in the nineteenth century because ships were required to travel via the Cape of Good Hope. In order to shorten the time in which despatches could be passed between Bombay and London, various overland routes were tried. One of these was the Alexandria to Suez pony express. Consequently, the Red Sea route became popular and a need arose for a refuelling station. Aden was considered as it is situated about halfway between Suez and Bombay and possessed an excellent sheltered port.

Negotiations were conducted between Commander Haines, Political Agent of the Bombay Government, and the Sultan of Lahej, the owner of Aden, for the port and environs. An agreement was made, but when it came to executing that agreement the Sultan's son refused. At this time a Madras ship, the *Duria Dowlat*, under British colours, was wrecked near Aden and the survivors were mistreated by the local Arabs while the cargo was plundered. This and the insults that had been heaped upon Haines and Britain by the Lahej Sultan were enough to cause the Bombay

Government to send some ships of the Honourable East India Company Navy to take the 'Rock' of Aden by force.

The ships sent were the Honourable East India Company's sloop of war *Coote*, schooner *Mahi* and barque *Anne Crichton*. Two Royal Navy vessels and troop transports were despatched from India to join Commander Haines. They were HMS *Volage*, HM Brig *Cruiser* and the transports *Lowjee Family* and *Ernaad*, which arrived on 16 January 1839. The troops on board were: The Bombay European Regiment; 24th Regiment Bombay Native Infantry; 4th Company of the 1st Battalion Artillery; and 6th Company (Golundauze) Artillery. Ten garrison guns were included for the defence of the port.

After a naval bombardment had silenced the Arab guns Aden was captured on 19 January 1839. With this successful action, Britain gained its first new territory under Queen Victoria. Aden was annexed as part of the Bombay Presidency. It also marked the beginning of a permanent military garrison. In May 1840 that garrison consisted of:

2 Battalion Artillery
Golundauze Battalion
Engineer Corps
HM 6th Regiment
Bombay European Regiment
10th Regiment Native Infantry
16th Regiment Native Infantry

During the first few years following the capture of Aden there were several attempts by the Arabs to recapture it. On each occasion the military garrison, with the help of the Red Sea Squadron of the Indian Navy, succeeded in repulsing the attacking tribesmen.

In 1858 a force composed of 2 or 3 companies of 57th Regiment, a Wing of the 29th Bombay Infantry and a detachment from the Hon. Company's Ship *Elphinstone*, defeated an Arab force at Sheikh Othman. Britain was now secure in Aden although a few further military actions took place.

The first of these was the Expedition to Shugra in December 1865 when trouble was experienced with the Fadhli tribe. The tribe had plundered a caravan within gunshot of the Aden fortifications. A detachment of 300 men of the 101st Grenadiers with a field force commanded by Colonel Woollcombe, C.B., Royal Artillery, attacked Bir and Asala, destroying the latter. They returned to Aden on 9 January 1866. Another expedition under the same commander was sent to Shugra on 14 March to destroy the town and forts, which was the principal stronghold of the Fadhli tribe. The Fadhli had captured a dhow under British protection, massacred the crew and sold the cargo. The British believed the Fadhli needed to be taught a lesson and a detachment of artillery, with two field pieces, and three companies of the 109th Infantry Regiment and some sappers were despatched by HMS *Lyra* and *Victoria*. The seamen and marines from the *Lyra*, about 40 in number, worked with the artillery. The town was destroyed on 15 March and the troops were back in Aden the following day.

A few years later, in 1873, a force of British and Indian infantry with three guns marched to Al Hauta (Lahej) to protect the Sultan against the Turks who had invaded his territory. After negotiations the Turkish troops were withdrawn.

OPERATIONS IN THE ADEN HINTERLAND AND THE ANGLO-TURKISH BOUNDARY COMMISSION

When the Turkish Army occupied the Yemen in 1872 it brought them into contact with the British on the Yemen/Aden Protectorate border. This ill-defined boundary became problematic for the British as Yemeni tribes enjoyed raiding into the Protectorate and had to be forcibly removed.

In 1901 tribal disputes arose in the Aden hinterland near the border. A group of hostile Arabs from Yemen constructed a defensible tower at Ad Dareja in Haushabi territory in 1900, which was under British protection. This tower commanded the main trade route and was used as a customs post garrisoned by 150 to 200 Turkish soldiers with reinforcements close to hand. Following failed diplomatic correspondence, it was destroyed in July by a force sent out from Aden, consisting of 200 men from 1st Battalion Royal West Kent Regiment, 200 men from 5th Bombay Light Infantry, half of No. 4 Company, Bombay Sappers and Miners, six mountain guns from No. 16 Company, Western Division, Royal Garrison Artillery and 20 members of Aden Troop.

In October 1901 the British and Turkish governments agreed to the demarcation of the frontier between Yemen and the Aden Protectorate. Both Turks and British would appoint a boundary commissioner to be escorted by no more than 200 men. The first meeting took place on 11 February 1902. From the very beginning the Turkish commissioners adopted an uncompromising attitude which bordered upon open hostility. In addition to putting forward preposterous claims, the Turks seized and occupied all territory in dispute. They also increased their garrison at Kataba, 12 miles from Dhala, and strengthened their post at Jalela, which was within 2 miles of the British commission's camp. The two Turkish garrisons totalled about 850 men, equipped with seven mountain guns and one modern field piece.

HM Government protests were ineffectual, the Sultan of Dhala appealing to Britain for assistance. In response to the increasing severity of the situation the Aden garrison was reinforced with the 102nd Prince of Wales Grenadiers, a Wing of the 123 Outram's Rifles and the Abbottabad Mountain Battery from India. In addition, the Aden Column was raised, comprising 2nd Royal Dublin Fusiliers, including a section of Maxim guns, 12 signallers, a double company of 102 Grenadiers, and two sections of field hospitals. The column left Sheikh Othman on 2 January 1903 with orders to 'watch' the frontier. The Aden garrison was not particularly strong and was further reinforced by the Hampshire Regiment, brought in from Lucknow, India. On arrival in Aden five companies were sent to Dhala. A field telegraph was built between Aden and Dhala, and the roads were improved. When the British felt secure enough, an ultimatum was presented to the Turkish government, which resulted in all Turkish troops and levies being withdrawn behind the line indicated by the British Commissioner as the approximate frontier of the Aden Protectorate. By March nearly 1,500 British and India soldiers were on the border. While the border was being surveyed Arab tribes launched numerous raids upon the surveying parties and British troops. A number of punitive actions were taken against Arab villages that supported the warlike tribesmen. The conditions suffered by the troops were very poor. Although casualties from fighting were not high, many suffered from malaria – in the case of the Hampshire's 75 percent of its strength were afflicted. The Hampshire's regimental history notes that camels provided the transport. Although some of the regiment had experienced camels and their ways on the Frontier in India, they discovered the Aden camel – and even more so its

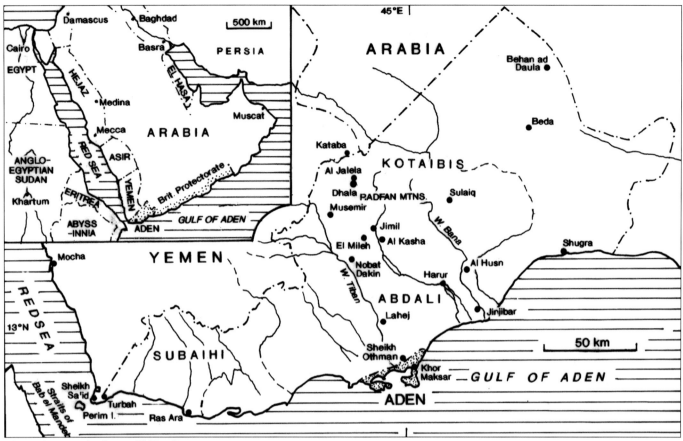

Aden and its Hinterland 1904. (Cliff Lord)

driver – to be far more intractable than those they had already encountered.

The following units were to see service with Aden Column, which was raised to provide the Boundary Commission's escort, protect survey parties, and to assist in the protection and building of roads in the hinterland:

102nd Grenadiers
94th Russell's Infantry
123rd Outram's Rifles
Hampshire Regiment
Buffs (Royal East Kent Regiment)
2nd Royal Dublin Fusiliers
30th Mountain Battery – later 110th (Abbottabad) Mountain Battery
Camel Battery of two 5-pdr guns drawn by camels and manned by the RGA from Aden
6 (British) Mountain Battery
45 Company RGA
Aden Troop
Section A., No. 16 British Field Hospital
Section A., No. 68 Native Field Hospital

When the Boundary Commission entered Subaihi territory a flying column was organised from the troops at Musemir, and a second force known as the Subaihi Column was mobilised at Aden to join them. On 1 March 1904 the Aden Column was broken up, although troops were temporarily retained at Dhala and along the line of communications. As the Boundary Commission approached the coast it used Ras Ara – 70 miles west of Aden – as its base, and 350 men from 94th Russell's Infantry were located there until the delimitation work was completed in May.

BRITISH MILITARY FORCES IN ADEN 1914–1919
Sheikh Said and Perim Island

Prior to their entry into the First World War, reports were received that the Turks were building up their forces in the Sheikh Said peninsula, Yemen, which was situated on the Straits of Bab El Mandib. Sheikh Said is only 18 kilometres from East Africa and two or three from Perim Island. Perim was a British Island opposite Sheikh Said in Yemen, and about 5 kilometres away was the Turkish stronghold of Fort Turbah. Perim was a small island invested with a small detachment of Indian forces not more than about 50 strong and was threatened by Fort Turbah. Gun emplacements were being built at Fort Turbah for a pair of Krupp guns which had a range that almost crossed the Red Sea to East Africa. Six field guns were also deployed locally as well. To add to this was about a Battalion sized unit of the Turkish Army. The Anglo-Indian Army recognised the threat that was posed by this situation and secret plans were made to destroy the fort by a convoy carrying 29 Infantry Brigade, which formed up in India. The convoy was to stop off at Aden and pick up 23 Sikh Pioneers, then work its way to Turbah. HMS Duke of Edinburgh protected the convoy armed with six 9.2 inch guns which were the main armament and ten 6 inch guns secondary armament. In the convoy was the 14 (King Georges Own) Sikhs, 69 Punjabis, 89 Punjabis and 1/6 Bn Gurkhas plus the 23 Sikhs picked up in Aden. Planned for the 10 of November 1914, the attack started with HMS Duke of Edinburgh shelling Turbah Fort and inflicting considerable damage. The convoy landed troops on the western side of Sheikh Said and covering fire was provided by HMS Duke of Edinburgh which had moved into position. The attack was successful and the Pioneers destroyed two Krupp guns, six field guns, and about 10,000 rounds of small arms ammunition, gun emplacements and huge quantities of artillery shells and cordite. Minimum casualties were encountered and later the convoy continued to Egypt. It was

7

not until 13 and 14 June 1915 that Perim Island was threatened again. About 300 shells were fired at the island from a field gun and a pair of smaller guns from shore. Dhows full of troops attacked Perim the following night. Only a few troops landed but made a hasty departure after a British Star Shell illuminated them.

THE WAR IN ADEN

Turkey entered the war on 5 November 1914, and a Turkish Army Corps under General Said Pasha was stationed in Yemen, which was a direct threat to the small and isolated garrison of Aden. The garrison comprised only one British and one Indian battalion, three companies of Royal Garrison Artillery, Aden Troop of 100 Indian Cavalry sowars, and 23 (Fortress) Company, Bombay Sappers and Miners. Said Pasha brought his troops within marching distance of Lahej. In March 1915, half a company of Baluchistan Infantry disembarked on its way to reinforce 6 Infantry Division in Mesopotamia. As the summer drew on it became obvious that the Turks intended to attack the protectorate. Major General D. L. B. Shaw commanding Aden Brigade decided to send some obsolete guns to Lahej to slow the enemy up with the new Moveable Column. Aden garrison was not ideal for defending the hinterland so the Moveable Column had been created and consisted of about 1,000 men. It had six 15-pounder and four 10-pounder guns manned by the Garrison Artillery. The newly arrived 4th Brecknockshire Battalion of the South Wales Borderers was a Territorial Battalion and was not trained up fully, but it had recently replaced the regular 1st Battalion Lancashire Fusiliers and joined in the Moveable Column. On 3 July they moved out and proceeded to march the seven miles to Sheikh Othman. Even the short distance was enough to put several of the Brecknocks down with heat exhaustion. The elements of the column included:

4th Battalion Brecknocks
15-pounder Camel Battery, Royal Garrison Artillery 6 guns
10-pounder Mountain Battery, Royal Garrison Artillery 4 guns
Most of 23 (Fortress) Company, Bombay Sappers and Miners
Company 23rd Sikh Pioneers including with two .450" machine guns and two .303" machine guns
Half Company 109th Infantry with two .450" machine guns and two .303" machine guns
2 Companies of 126th Baluchistan Infantry.

All the spare motor transport from Aden was used to send the machine guns and gunners ahead. Turkey had 2,000 men marching on Lahej with six guns and had the cooperation of the local Arabs. The Moveable Column moved out toward Lahej on 3 July. Many of the troops suffered severely from the heat, particularly the Brecknocks. The camel drivers cut their loads and fled when fired upon, and the stores, water and guns were left in the sand four miles from Lahej along with the 15 pounder-guns. A detachment of 126th Baluch, 109th Infantry and 100 men of the Brecknocks who were still capable of holding a rifle repelled all attacks until dawn on 5 July. Then a retirement began from Bir Nasir. They were in no condition to fight a sustained defence. When they had recovered all the wounded men they made their way back to Sheikh Othman where there was plenty of water. Very quickly a decision was made to fall back to Khormaksar seven miles away where the Royal Navy could give enfilading fire. Losing Sheikh Othman was a blow to the British because the majority of fresh water for Aden was taken from there and he ships in port were now obliged

to condense water for the town. Reinforcements were called in from Egypt and arrived very quickly. Half the 108th Infantry arrived on 8 July with the 4th Buffs who relieved the Brecknocks. Ten days later the 28th (Frontier Force) Indian Infantry Brigade under Major General Sir G. J. Younghusband arrived from Egypt. Altogether the following units of 28th Infantry Brigade were: 51st Sikhs, 53rd Sikhs, 56th Punjabis, and there were two non-regular batteries of the Berkshire Battery, Royal Horse Artillery (T) and "B" Battery Honourable Artillery Company. Major General Younghusband assumed the post of Governor and Commander in Chief in Aden. He despatched his Brigade under the command of Lieutenant Colonel A.M.S. Elsmie, 56th Punjab Rifles, to recapture Sheikh Othman on 21 July. Elsmie was supported by Aden Garrison including a detachment of 23 (Fortress) Company, and Aden Troop. Turkish troops in Lahej were surprised and routed. Several hundred prisoners were taken. Major General Stewart now replaced Major General Younghusband. The town was secured and the water supply was resumed in Aden. There continued to be success on 24 August when the enemy garrison at Fiyush was forced to retire on Lahej temporarily. Four days later a similar success was gained at Waht, but again only temporarily. During the rest of the year further skirmishes occurred with the infantry averting a threatened advance upon Imad. When Major General Stewart requested more troops it was approved, but he was told to wait until more troops became available in East Africa though he was not restricted from an active defence. This included protecting the railway up to Robat. Small reinforcements continued to arrive and included 5 Company Bengal Sappers and Miners who started work on 1 September. A Territorial howitzer battery disembarked at Maala on 11 September followed up by a Camel Corps on 14 September. The 26th (King George's Own) Light Cavalry, Indian Army, arrived on 20 September. However, the defence of Aden was weakened in the middle of September by the recall of 28th Infantry Brigade. Now it was the time for active defence and to see the Turks to be harried and attacked, but there was no permanent advance to the Waht-Fiyush line. During 1916, the Movable Column inflicted considerable loss on the Turkish force near Subar, thus securing the tribes to the east. On 16 March 1916 the Turks attacked Imad in force but were beaten off without difficulty. Later that year, on 7 December the Turkish posts at Jabir and Marhat were attacked, with the enemy suffering about 200 casualties. That same year the seaplane carriers HMS *Raven II* and *Ben My Chree* arrived with aircraft undertaking bombing and reconnaissance flights. The aircraft were of immense value despite only being on station for a short time. Further skirmishing was to take place for the next two years, with the cavalry able to attack quickly and make a hasty retreat. Bombardment by the Royal Navy was also used from time to time if ememy came within reach of their guns. The 26th Indian Light Cavalry and Aden Troop came into their own but the latter of which were down to 80 men. In 1917 a number of aircraft of the RFC were sent to Aden where they took part in raids on enemy positions and reconnaissance tasks. The units were half a Flight of No. 114 Squadron RFC and No. 51 Kite Section RFC. Thus the war continued until an armistice was called. Said Pasha, the Turkish military commander was in no hurry to surrender after the armistice of 11 November 1918 until long negotiations were completed on 6 December 1918. Although it could be argued that the Turkish blockade of Aden throughout the war was a major success, it was British policy to employ a smaller and, at first, less well armed force to keep a larger Turkish force tied down in Lahej for the duration of the war to prevent them causing trouble in Yemen.

Indian Army Order No. 618-1916 stated that the title of the GOC Aden (Independent) Brigade would change to GOC Aden. It also stated the infantry brigade and its various attached units, forming the Movable Column, would be known as "the Aden Infantry Brigade". The troops under the command of the GOC Aden would be known as the Aden Field Force.

MILITARY RAILWAY

A military railway was built by Royal Engineers in 1915–16 from the Port of Aden to Sheikh Othman and later extended further north towards Lahej in 1919. The railway was available to the public from 1922. Material was obtained from the Bombay, Baroda and Central India Railway and the Eastern Bengal Railway. Forty-seven kilometres of line was built from Maala to Sheikh Othman in 1916, Sheikh Othman to Lahej in 1919 and Lahej to El Khudad in 1920. It is reported to have had seven narrow gauge locomotives and one railcar. On May 7, 1920 the Government of India transferred the railway from military control to that of the 'Railway Board' in India creating the 'Aden State Railway' under the control of Mr Affleck who was designated 'Engineer-in-Charge'. In 1922 the line was made available for public use, carrying traffic between Aden and El Khudad and supplies to the military outpost at Sheikh Othman. The line was run by the Indian North Western Railway under a designated Engineer-in-Charge. Proving too expensive to maintain the railway was closed in 1929 before being dismantled in 1930.

UNITS THAT SERVED IN ADEN 1914–1919
Royal Flying Corps
½ Flight No. 114 Squadron RFC
No. 57 Kite Balloon Section RFC

CAVALRY
26th Indian Cavalry
Aden Troop (Punjabis)

ARTILLERY
61 Company RGA (Coastal Artillery)
62 Company RGA
69 Company RGA
70 Company RGA (Coastal Artillery)
76 Company, RGA (Coastal Artillery)
85 Company, RGA
10-pdr Camel Battery, RGA
15-pdr Camel Battery, RGA
5" battery, RGA
2/1/Devon (H) Battery
4/Hants (H) Battery
1105(H) Battery
Malay States Guides Mountain Battery
Aden Ammunition Column.

ENGINEERS
5 Company, Bengal Sappers and Miners
6 Engineer Field Park, Bengal Sappers and Miners
23 (Fortress) Company, 3 Bombay Sappers and Miners
51 Company, 1st Bengal Sappers and Miners
Aden Defence Light Section, Bombay Sappers and Miners

SIGNALS
Aden Signal Company, Bombay Sappers and Miners
½ Troop, Pack Wireless.

INFANTRY
1/Royal Irish Rifles
1/Lancs
1/Brecknock South Wales Borderers
4/Buffs
4th Duke of Cornwall's Light Infantry
6/East Surreys
7/Hampshires
1st Brahmans
7th Rajput
23rd Sikh Pioneers (from 29 Brigade)
33rd Punjabis
38th Dogras
45 (Aden) Rifles
62nd Punjabis (from 28 Brigade)
69th Punjabis
75th Carnatics
2/101st Grenadiers
108th Infantry
109th Infantry
126th Baluchis (from 30 Brigade)
Malay States Guides
1st Yemen Infantry
Aden Machine Gun Company

MEDICAL SERVICES
2 Section, British General Hospital
No. 10 British Stationary Hospital
No. 10 Advanced Depot of Medical Stores
No. 10 British Staging Section Casualty Clearing Station
Section B, No. 24 British Field Ambulance
Section B, No. 26 British Field Ambulance
Section A, No. 26 Indian General Hospital
Section B, No. 26 Indian General Hospital
No. 80 Indian Stationary Hospital
No. 80 Indian Staging Section Casualty Clearing Station
2 sections 105 Indian Field Ambulance, plus 1 British section
Section C, No. 133 Indian Field Ambulance
Section D, No. 133 Indian Field Ambulance
Section A, No. 138 Indian Field Ambulance
Section B, No. 138 Indian Field Ambulance
Section A, No. 138 Combined Field Ambulance
Section B, No. 138 Combined Field Ambulance
No. 138 Combined Field Ambulance
Benares Ambulance Transport Section

VETERINARY SERVICES
Field Veterinary Section

SUPPLY AND TRANSPORT
Supply and Transport Office
Detachment 7 Mule Corps
18 Pack Corps (became 18 Pack Mule Corps in 1921)
25 Camel Corps
56 Camel Company (Siladar)
Aden Mechanical Transport Section
Aden Local Transport

Aden Labour Corps
Porter Corps
Aden Water Column
No. 31 Divisional Supply Company
No. 53 Brigade Supply Section
No. 55 Supply and Transport HQ (Line of Communication)
No. 108 Brigade Supply Section
'T' Supply Depot Company
91 Supply Section
92 Supply Section
321 Supply Section
46 Supply Workshop Section
631 Bakery Section
634 Bakery Section
7 Cattle Purchasing Section
150 Supply Tally Section

ORDNANCE

Ordnance Field Park
Ordnance Advance Depot
Detachment Indian Ordnance Depot

TEMPORARY TROOPS

28 (Frontier Force) Indian Brigade, comprising:
51st Sikhs
53rd Sikhs
56th Punjabis
62nd Punjabis

Berkshire Battery, RHA (T)
'B' Battery Honourable Artillery Company

29 Indian Brigade, comprising:
57th Rifles
Patiala Infantry
23rd Sikh Pioneers

30 Indian Brigade:
½ 126th Baluchis
Australian Light Horse (disembarked from troop ship for short period)
9th Gurkha Rifles (double company disembarked from troop ship for short period)
Machine Gun Detachment, and Wireless Section, HMS *Philomel*

TURKISH YEMEN ARMY CORPS, 1916

In February 1916 the principal units of the Turkish Army in Yemen were:

39th Division, Taiz
115th Infantry Regiment
116th Infantry Regiment (part)
117th Infantry Regiment
119th Infantry Regiment (part)
7th Model Battalion

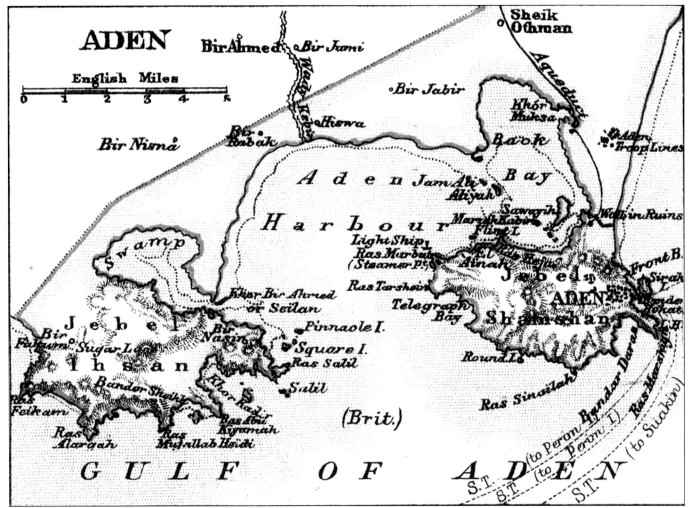

Aden 1914–1918. (Map by David Birtles)

40th Division, Hodeida
  118th Infantry Regiment
  119th Infantry Regiment (part)
  120th Infantry Regiment

Corps Troops
  26th Cavalry Regiment
  Horse artillery battalion
  3 machine gun companies
  9 field and mountain batteries
  Howitzer battery
  4 heavy batteries
  7th Engineer Battalion
  Independent Engineer Company
  Rocket Battery
  There also were a large number of Arab auxiliaries and two militia battalions

The following Turkish units were in the Protectorate in 1916:

LAHEJ

  1st Battalion, 117th Infantry Regiment
  Elements of 26th Cavalry Regiment
  A number of guns

WAHT

  2nd Battalion, 115th Infantry Regiment
  3rd Battalion, 115th Infantry Regiment
  3rd Battalion, 116th Infantry Regiment
  2nd Battalion, 117th Infantry Regiment
  3rd Battalion, 117th Infantry Regiment
  Machine Gun Company (5 machine guns)
  Independent Engineer Company
  Battery of 4 x 7.7cm guns and 1 mortar attached
  Battery of 2 x howitzers
  2 mountain batteries (one probably Quick Firing)

SUBAR

  3rd Battalion, 119th Infantry Regiment
  7th Model Battalion
  2 x machine guns
  Mountain battery

SHEIKH SAID

  1st Battalion, 120th Regiment
  Mountain battery
  Half-battery of two 10.5cm guns

ROYAL NAVAL AIR SERVICE IN THE PROTECTORATE

The Royal Naval Air Service was the air arm of the Royal Navy, and came under the Admiralty's Air Department, which existed from 1 July 1914 to 1 April 1918, when it was merged with the British Army's Royal Flying Corps to form the Royal Air Force.

The authorities in Aden requested aircraft for the defence of Aden in 1916 as the Protectorate had had an advancing Turkish force to contend with since July 1915, that had already occupied Lahej some 20 miles north of Aden. Both British and Indian troops of Aden Garrison were capable of keeping the Turks out of Aden, but there was concern that the local tribes would join the Turks, consequently providing the Turks with the advantage to press home their advance on Aden port. Tribal leaders met Ali

Said Pasha, the Turkish commander, in the spring of 1916. As the Turkish force in Yemen was isolated from their army in the north by the hostile Arab *Idrissi* they were dependent on the local tribes for most of their supplies. The authorities in Aden thought a show of force would help prevent the local tribes from siding with the Turks, but the heat was not ideal for British troops to advance in. A surprise air raid on Turkish positions was deemed the best solution. A converted freighter to a seaplane carrier, the *Ben-my-Chree*, was refitting in Port Said, Egypt, and transferred her aircraft to another seaplane carrier, the *Raven II*. Aircraft embarked were one two-seater Short seaplane and five Sopwith Schneider seaplanes. Perim Island was selected as the ideal place to erect her seaplanes, which were then stowed on deck in a ready-to-fly mode, then entered Aden Harbour at night on 30 March 1916. A reconnaissance of the enemy was made at dawn on 1 April, which was followed by a bombing mission. In three days, 91 twenty-pound bombs were dropped from low altitudes on the main Turkish camps near Subar, Waht and Fiyush. Pamphlets were also dropped urging the local tribes to desert the Turks. *Raven II* departed Aden on 3 April after a very successful mission. Further air operations were conducted in June 1916 by the seaplane carrier *Ben-my-Chree* (Ben-my-Chree is Manx for 'girl of my heart'). While approaching Aden on 7 June at dawn, a Short seaplane was despatched on a reconnaissance of the Lahej area. Military camps north of Lahej were selected along with a depot and camp near Subar. Trench and gun positions were observed and recorded and over the next six days bombing sorties were made twice daily at dawn and dusk. A total of forty-four 112-pound bombs were dropped from heights under 1,000 feet. On 12 June petrol bombs were dropped on Subar camp which caused a huge fire. *Ben-my-Chree* departed for Perim Island that afternoon. Bombing sorties were made on 13 June on the Turkish camps at Jebel Malu and Jebel Akrabi. A wireless-fitted Sopwith spotted for the seaplane carrier's guns firing on the camps. This concluded the operations against the Turkish advance on Aden.

ADEN COMMAND (ROYAL AIR FORCE) 1928

RAF COMMANDERS IN ADEN

ADEN COMMAND
  1928 Group Captain W.G.S. Mitchell
  1931 Group Captain O.T. Boyd
  1934 Group Captain C.F.A. Portal (Air Commodore from January 1935)
  1935 Air Vice-Marshal E.L. Gossage

BRITISH FORCES ADEN
  1936 Air Commodore W.A. McClaughry
  1938 Air Vice-Marshal G.R.M. Reid
  1941 Air Vice-Marshal F.G.D. Hards
  1943 Air Vice-Marshal F.H. MacNamara (RAAF)
  1945 Air Vice-Marshal H.T. Lydford
  1948 Air Vice-Marshal A.C. Stevens
  1950 Air Vice-Marshal F.J. Fressanges
  1952 Air Vice-Marshal D. Macfadyen
  1953 Air Vice-Marshal S.O. Bufton
  1955 Air Vice-Marshal L.F. Sinclair

BRITISH FORCES ARABIAN PENINSULA
  1957 Air Vice-Marshal M.L. Heath
  1959 Air Chief Marshal Sir Hubert Patch

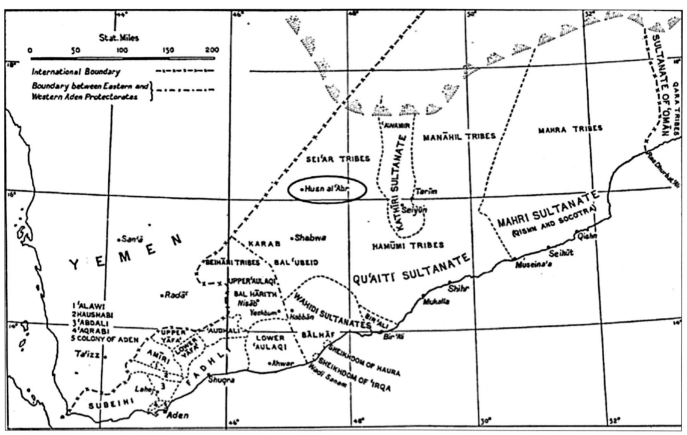

Aden and the Protectorate. (Map by David Birtles)

Parade and games in honour of Air Vice-Marshal Sir Sam Elworthy (Middle East Command). L to R Amir Omar, The heir apparent Amir Ghalib, H.H. Sultan 'Awadh bin Saleh al Qu'aiti, Arthur Francis Watts (British Agent and Resident Adviser), Air Vice-Marshal Sir Sam Elworthy. Mukalla Palace Courtyard, ca later 1962 or 1963. (Sultan Ghalib)

1960 Air Marshal Sir Charles Elworthy

COMMANDERS (AIR FORCE) MIDDLE EAST

1959 Air Chief Marshal D.J. Pryer Lee
1961 Air Chief Marshal F. Rosier
1963 Air commodore J.E. Johnson
1965 Air Vice-Marshal A.H. Humphrey

On its establishment in 1928, Aden Command was a RAF command responsible for the control of all British armed forces in the Aden Protectorate, and later renamed British Forces in Aden in 1936, and renamed again in 1956 as British Forces Arabian Peninsula. In 1959 Middle East Command was split into two commands. The two commands were British Forces Arabian Peninsula based at Aden, and Middle East Command in Cyprus, which in 1961 was renamed Near East Command. In 1961 the command was renamed, again, this time as Middle East Command Aden. With the withdrawal from Aden in 1967, the remaining British Forces in the Arabian Peninsula, which included units at Salalah in Oman and Masirah, were reorganised under Headquarters British Forces Gulf at RAF Muharraq in Bahrain.

AIR CONTROL

Air Control, or the use of aircraft to subdue the population, was implemented by the RAF in the Aden Protectorate to provide a projection of governmental power (law and order) at a low cost,

Table 3: British Military Forces in Aden 1939–45 (excluding locally raised forces)

2/5th Mahratta Light Infantry	left Aden in August 1940 and arrived at Port Sudan on 23 August
1/2nd Punjab Regiment	arrived in Aden in May 1940. Moved to British Somaliland on 29 June 1940, returning to Aden on 18 August
3/15th Punjab Regiment	arrived in Aden in July 1940. Served in British Somaliland from July until 16 August 1940, when it returned to Aden
2nd Battalion, The Black Watch	arrived at Khormaksar on 1 July 1940. Served in British Somaliland from 6 – 19 August 1940 and returned to Aden. Left Aden for Suez on 26 August
1st Battalion, Northern Rhodesia Regiment	withdrawn from British Somaliland on 16 August 1940, remaining in Aden until 17 September
3/7th Rajput Regiment	arrived in Aden during August 1940, left the following month. Returned in December 1942, remaining until May 1944
2/10th Gurkha Rifles	May – December 1942
3/1st Punjab Regiment	arrived in November 1942, relocated to Socotra in April 1943
Mewar Bhopal Infantry (Indian State Forces)	December 1942 – May 1944
1st Rampur Infantry (Indian State Forces)	May – November 1944
1st Hyderabad Lancers (Indian State Forces)	November 1944 – December 1945
1st Patiala Lancers (Indian State Forces)	December 1945 – 1946
Somaliland Camel Corps	withdrawn from British Somaliland on 16 August 1940 and sent to Aden. Left Aden by 17 September 1940
Bikanir Ganga Risala (Indian State Forces) Camel unit	sent to Aden from India on 8 September 1940, returning in 1942
HQRA Aden	1 March 1944 – 31 December 1944
5th Heavy Regiment, RA	formed 8 September 1939 in Aden
9th (Minden) Heavy Battery, RA	
15th AA Battery, Hong Kong Singapore Royal Artillery	formed 8 September 1939
23rd AA Battery, HKSRA	arrived 23 February 1940 from Singapore. This battery served in British Somaliland from 6 – 16 August 1940
24th Searchlight Battery, HKSRA	formed 30 March 1940
9th Coast Battery	14 December 1940 – 17 May 1945
9th Coast Battery South Arabian	17 May – 31 December 1945
5th Coast Regiment	14 December 1940 – 1 March 1944. Reformed as 1st Heavy Anti-Aircraft Artillery Regiment, HKSRA The AA batteries became HAA batteries on 1 June 1940
18th Mountain Battery, Indian Army	left India for Aden on 23 October 1940
27th Mountain Battery, Indian Army	raised in India 1 December 1939 and moved to Aden. Left Aden for East Africa during August 1940
20th Fortress Company, RE	
Detachment Royal Indian Army Service Corps	
17th Indian Staging Section	

which would save manpower and casualties to both sides. Air power was thought to be able to provide internal security in areas with a lack of roads and vast tracts of remote mountains. This proved to be very successful from the mid-1920s until the early 1950s. Costs and casualties were dramatically reduced. Britain had control of the air and a highly trained and efficient air force. This, with strong rules of engagement, enabled the RAF to be able to punish wayward tribes over the next 30 years. The rules of engagement by the RAF were quite straightforward. Once trouble was detected, which could have been the raiding of caravans through the passes, the decision of guilt was determined and a fine placed on the tribe. Should the fine not be paid then the tribe's houses and fortifications were photographed and identified correctly. A day's warning was given that bombing would commence if the fine was

RAF parade being inspected at RAF Khormaksar 1943. Note the topee flash which is in RAF colours. (Sean Brady)

not paid and that they should evacuate the area. If there was no response, then another notice was given by air one hour before the air raid. Failure to respond would then trigger the RAF to destroy the equivalent or approximate worth of tribal property as the fine. This approach was acceptable to the tribes and seen as fair. After the air raid the tribe would then be able to go back to their village and repair the damage. No casualties were incurred providing the tribesmen took notice of the warnings. The work of the RAF was backed up by Political Officers and a limited military presence. Without a doubt this policy worked very well indeed in the short term, but no real attempt was made to provide long-term solutions to the problems. Eventually the RAF did enjoy some respect when they delivered famine relief and medical supplies to the tribes in times of need. When the tribes became politicised with the spread of Arab nationalism in the 1950s the validity of Air Control was suddenly in question. It was no longer a case of frightening a few tribesmen and blowing up a house or two, but the bombing of military targets either in Yemen or in the Western Aden Protectorate. Political pressure was brought to bear on the British Government by the UN when a fort in Yemen was attacked after repeated incursions by Yemeni aircraft into the Protectorate. Political pressure from Arab Nationalists and the Eastern Bloc had a profound effect on British strategy and Air Control as the main arm of control diminished. A notable turning point was the inability of the RAF to effectively influence the outcome of the abandonment of the Government Guards' fort at Robat in 1955, when under attack by the local Shams tribes. The RAF relinquished command of the APL and internal security to the Army in 1957. This new strategy was seen as less internationally embarrassing.

By placing more troops on the ground, both Arab and British (plus air to ground support by the RAF), it was inevitable that it would be more costly and that there would be a huge increase in casualties. The new strategy might have been effective if there had been a long-term plan for conflict termination once military action had taken place, as in the Radfan. Once a battle was won on the ground the Army moved out only to have the vacuum filled by dissident tribesmen once again. This was a political failure rather than a military failure.

BRITISH MILITARY FORCES IN ADEN 1939

HQ BRITISH TROOPS ADEN, 3 SEPTEMBER 1939

HQ Royal Artillery Aden
Detachment, 8th Anti-Aircraft Battery, Royal Artillery
9th Heavy Battery, RA
20th Fortress Company, RE
2/5th Mahratta Light Infantry – Khormaksar
Aden Protectorate Levies – Khormaksar
Independent Flight Armoured Cars, RAF

This information was kindly prepared by David A. Ryan.

POST-SECOND WORLD WAR: 1945–1963

After the end of the Second World War the Military Base in Aden was reduced in military personnel. Sporadic fighting continued to take place on the border with Yemen and the system of Air Control as the strategy for containment of tribes continued. The RAF provided famine relief in the Eastern Aden Protectorate

A sniper firing his British made No. 4 Mk I (T) rifle with the No. 32 telescope in the Radfan. The sling is a US leather sling. (Sean Brady)

in 1948 and all was quiet there, however problems still continued with the tribes in the Western Aden Protectorate. No. 20 Wing, RAF Regiment, comprising of 58 and 66 Rifle Squadrons with a strength of about 300 officers and airmen, was despatched to Aden in 1948. The purpose of the Wing was to provide internal security and an anti-riot role within Aden Colony. It was also tasked with reinforcing Somaliland in an emergency, and to provide protection of an airstrip at Mweiga, Kenya. The Wing also put down Arab Somali riots at the new oil refinery at Aden. There was unrest in Dhala in 1947 and in Sagladi territory in 1948. Acting Flt Lt G. Gallagher RAF APL was awarded the Military Cross for bravery during these actions. Many more awards were to be given before the Emergency was declared at the end of 1963. The APL was given additional responsibility from 1952 until September 1953 to support the Trucial Oman Levies. With the rise of Arab nationalism that spread right across the Arab world the tribes in the Protectorates became politicised. No longer was it a question of tribesmen wanting to steal from passing caravans, but major raids by well-armed, and sometimes well-trained gangs of men. A number of minor actions took place in the early 1950s, but in April 1955 the total Trained Force was sent to the Wadi Hatib for 8 days on offensive operations in an attempt to relive the

A Rifleman from 1 East Anglian Regiment prepares to deliver water to outposts. Local tribesmen were charted to deliver food water and ammunition to the troops operating high in the Radfan Mountains. The outposts were to disrupt dissidents that were threatening the Aden Dhala trade route. (Sean Brady)

Coldstream Guards firing a General Purpose Machine Gun (GPMG) in the mountains of the WAP January 1965. (Joint Public Relations Unit Aden)

An 84 Squadron RAF Beverley aircraft up-country in WAP. (Sean Brady)

Saladin armoured cars of D Squadron, 4 Royal Tank Regiment, after a successful night operation east of the Dhala Thumier road on 6 May 1964. (Joint Public Relations Unit Aden)

operational strain on the Force. The dissidents adopted typically sound guerrilla tactics and disengaged. It was a moral victory for the APL but little more. Soon after, a somewhat complacent Britain was shocked by one particular event. A routine relieve of the Government Guard fort at Robat from Nisab was ambushed with serious loss of life in 1955. Prior to this ambush the convoy had been run 25 times and resulted in 37 APL casualties plus many Government Guards. However, on this occasion the APL had two British officers, one Arab officer and two soldiers killed. Five men were wounded. The Government Guard lost three men killed, two wounded and two surrendered. Analysis of the ambush left little doubt that the dissidents had become almost immune to area strafing and bombing. The increased number of dissidents, with their vastly increased ammunition supply from the Yemen

had now made a successful penetration of the Wadi Hatib. Prior to this ambush there had been a high APL desertion rate and a shortage of trained men. The APL was undermanned for the tasks required, and many of the men were tired from previous action. This loss of life was perhaps the major wake-up call required to reorganise the APL and increase its size.

During the period 1954 to 1957, the APL while under RAF control, was involved in the following actions:

The defeat of over 400 Yemeni soldiers and 2,000 tribesmen blocking the border route to Fort Manawa in the Wadi Habib, Beihan

The quelling of a revolt by Shaari tribesmen near Dhala; Many rebels killed and 49 taken prisoners

Successful opening of an important trade route north from Mafidh previously closed over a long period by hostile tribesmen

Halting of border raids in the Mertaa – Amm Soma locality

Capture of a complete band of 22 dissidents at Mukeiras

Operations off Dhala – Fort Thumia road in the Radfan against rebel tribesmen

Numerous engagements while proceeding to and from the relief of forts on various parts of the West Aden Protectorate, Robat, Am Kedah, Khaura, Mertaa

Anti gun-runner patrols in the Ramlat Sabatein, Shabwa and South West Rub al Kali areas

Aid to Civil Power during civil disturbances in Aden Colony

Site location and construction of several operational airstrips in the WAP

Protection for HE The Governor of Aden while on a prolonged visit to Mukeiras and Garrison duties at Mukeiras, Dhala, Ataq and Beihan

With Army control in 1957, many more operations were to take place with at least eight in 1957. Testament to the intensity of the operations lies in the number of awards for this period prior to the Emergency. As a consequence, there was an increasing use of British infantry, artillery and armoured cars to help support the APL and Government Guard. By the early 1960s there were fewer incidents. The APL was handed over to the Federal Government as the Federal Regular Army on 30 November 1961. Gradually the dissidents infiltrated the Western Aden Protectorate more and more with Yemeni and Egyptian backing. By the end of 1963 the Aden Emergency was declared.

BRITISH MILITARY FORCES IN ADEN 1964–67 (THE STATE OF EMERGENCY)

In 1963 an insurgent organisation named the National Liberation Front (NLF) was created. Enjoying backing from Egypt, the organisation's headquarters were in Taiz, Yemen. On 14 October 1963 a decision was made to shift from a policy based on politics to one of violent 'revolutionary struggle'. This became clear when a bomb attack occurred against the High Commissioner and Federal ministers at Khormaksar Airport on 10 December

Major General J H Cubbon, with HBL Commandant Pat Grey, stops to talk to one of the HBL legionaries while inspecting the HBL parade, ca 1963/64. (Dhow Magazine)

In 1958, 33 Parachute Light Regiment RA sent C Troop, 97 (Lawson's Company) Para Bty, to Aden. The unit was issued with five 75mm M1 Pack Howitzers, which were redesignated M116 in 1962. One gun was a reserve/maintenance gun. The unit remained in Aden for nearly two years. (Joint Public Relations Unit Aden)

A British official inspecting a guard of honour of the Kings Own Scottish Borderers around 1963. (Dhow Magazine)

East Anglian soldiers with their 3-inch mortar, Mk 5 barrel and Mk 5 bipod in the Radfan. (Sean Brady)

Members of 3 Para in the Radfan Mountains in 1964. (Joint Public Relations Unit Aden)

A machine gunner with a GPMG firing at a target in the desert with assistance from a spotter. (Sean Brady)

A 105mm pack howitzer from J Battery, 3 Light Regiment, Royal Horse Artillery, in action in close support of Federal troops in the Beihan district, close to the Yemen border in 1964. (Sean Brady)

Marines from Y Company 45 Commando inspect the damage immediately after a Westland Scout Helicopter crashed at Drumbeat on Operation Tamar in Area West, up-country. (Sean Brady)

1963. A State of Emergency was declared which lasted until the British left at the end of 1967. By this time Aden had become a very important military base.

In 1960 Headquarters Middle East Command had located itself there and four years later 24 Infantry Brigade was to move to Little Aden after relocating from Kenya. The NLF's insurgents infiltrated across the border, into South Arabia, where they were tasked with creating mayhem throughout the country. Their path was prepared by a propaganda war run by Egypt using Cairo Radio, and two radio stations in Yemen, Radio Sana and Radio Taiz. Clever and entertaining programs were transmitted to the people of South Arabia, which gradually indoctrinated them into the politics of Egypt and Arab nationalism. The nationalists also

encouraged tribesmen to take up arms against government forces by bribing them with new rifles. This subversion was increasingly successful, government forces suffering many attacks on border forts while convoys on the Dhala Road frequently encountered both landmines and ambushes. British and Federal forces quickly drew up a plan to combat these problems.

This became known as the Radfan Campaign, being named after the Radfan Mountains where the dissidents were gathered. An ad hoc brigade-strength formation, known as RADFORCE, was cobbled together. Its brief was to place troops in the Radfan area and evict the warring tribesmen, denying them access to fertile areas, and their routes to the Yemen. Consisting essentially of mountain warfare, operations began on 30 April 1964. On 11

An RAF Beverley crippled by a mine on Habilayn airstrip in June 1967. (Peter Herrett)

Coldstream Guards in the Western Aden Protectorate 1966 with an 81mm mortar. (Sean Brady)

NLF eventually took control. Without a doubt, the terrorist propaganda and intimidation was very successful. Nevertheless, British and Federal forces succeeded in curbing terrorism and enabled the British Government to negotiate from a position of some strength.

Aden Brigade was responsible for internal security in Aden State, while 24 Infantry Brigade, stationed in Little Aden, was given the task of providing forces for 'up-country' within the Federation, although they could be called on to assist in Aden. The military forces in Aden State performed a policeman's role under very different circumstances to their colleagues 'up-country'. They had to cope with urban terrorism as opposed to the campaign in the Radfan, which resembled soldiering on the old North West Frontier of India. Considerable restraint and discipline was shown by all, without which a successful withdrawal in November 1967 would not have been possible.

COMMANDS AND FORMATIONS

HQ Middle East Command (HQ MEC) moved to Aden 1 March 1961. Disbanded 29 November 1967.

Aden Brigade – served as Aden garrison.

39 Brigade – HQ arrived from Northern Ireland on 11 May 1964 and took command of units already in Aden. Returned to UK during October 1964.

24 Brigade – HQ arrived from East Africa during October 1964, while its units went home. Took over units of 39 Brigade.

THE WITHDRAWAL FROM ADEN
11 October 1967 – 25 January 1968
Operation Magister (Naval Task Force 318)

Increased terrorist attacks and continued civil disturbances saw the situation in Aden quickly deteriorate. Heavy fighting broke out between rival terrorist groups and the British forces gradually moved back to defensive positions by 24 September. This was known as the Scrubber Line and was slightly north of RAF Khormaksar. Naval forces started to assemble off Aden in early

May 1964, 39 Brigade took over from RADFORCE, when the former's headquarters was flown in from Northern Ireland.

By 11 June the campaign was over. During October the brigade was replaced by 24 Brigade. Although the Radfan Campaign was a military success for the British, worldwide press coverage provided much hostile propaganda against Britain and the Federation. Although trouble continued to flare up, both on the border and in the mountains, it was on a lesser scale after the Radfan Campaign. Nationalist organisations also chose to support a campaign of terrorism in Aden. The 1964 British declaration which stated that they would leave Aden 'not later than 1968' caused the various nationalist bodies to vie for power, each hoping they would be the rulers of the country following Britain's withdrawal. The major terrorist organisations were FLOSY and the NLF Although FLOSY was very strong in Aden State, the

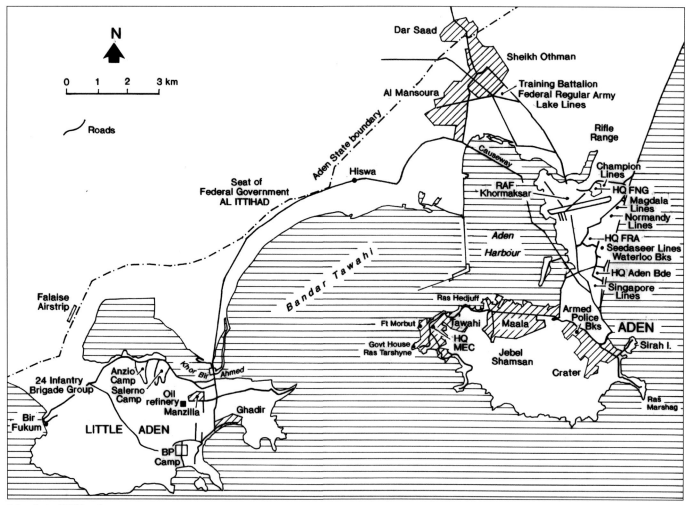

Aden State. (Cliff Lord)

Landing Craft RPL07 (Ramp Powered Lighter) of the Joint Services Port Squadron at sea off Aden 1965. (Sean Brady)

A Royal Air Force Wessex helicopter carrying a 105mm Pack Howitzer of 19 Regiment, RA as it hovers over the flight deck of HMS *Bulwark* during exercises off the coast of South Arabia. (Sean Brady)

Table 4: Royal Navy Warships at the Evacuation of Aden in 1967 – Task Force 318 (Operation Magister) 11 October 1967 to 25 January 1968

Aircraft carriers	HMS *Eagle*, HMS *Hermes*
Commando carriers	HMS *Albion*, HMS *Bulwark*
Assault Ships	HMS *Fearless*, HMS *Intrepid*
Guided Missile Destroyers	HMS *London*, HMS *Devonshire*
Destroyer	HMS *Barrosa*
Frigates	HMS *Ajax*, HMS *Phoebe*, HMS *Minerva*
Submarine	HMS *Auriga*
Minesweeper	HMS *Appleton*
RFA support ships	*Dewdale, Appleleaf, Olna, Stromness, Retainer, Resurgent, Fort Sandusky, Tidespring, Tideflow*
Landing ship (logistic)	*Sir Galahad*

October. The Royal Navy ensured the final part of the withdrawal from Aden was successful. Twenty-four Royal Naval ships participated. Air protection of the fleet was provided by aircraft carrier HMS Eagle which had Blackburn Buccaneer carrier-borne attack aircraft and the de Havilland DH 110 Sea Vixen two-seat carrier-based fleet air-defence fighter flying air patrols. The ship's Type 984 radar provided excellent early warning and control of flight operations. Naval Air Squadrons 820 and 848 provided support to the ground forces. Evacuation proceeded on 26 November 1967 starting with Crater, Steamer Point and Ma'alla. A massive airlift was also in progress. Aden Garrison was also evacuated in good order, and in the last week of November, the remaining 3,500 men of the British garrison were evacuated. On 28 November at 15:00

HMS *Eskimo*, a Tribal-class frigate off the coast of Aden 1967. (Joint Public Relations Unit Aden)

all British units were out of Aden but the task force remained on station until midnight when independence was officially declared for the People's Republic of Southern Yemen. On 7 December HMS *Bulwark* arrived, relieving HMS *Albion*, and three days later sailed to Masirah along with an escort of destroyers HMS *Devonshire* and HMS *Barrosa*. For some months a small naval task force remained offshore to provide assistance for British Embassy staff and British nationals at the British Petroleum oil refinery located at Little Aden.

2
THE ARMED FORCES OF ADEN

1st YEMEN INFANTRY

Turkish troops based at Lahej during the First World War posed a serious threat to the port of Aden, and a Movable Column of British and Indian troops was employed in harassing the Turkish force. Captain M.C. Lake (later Lieutenant Colonel Lake, CMG, OBE) of the 101st Grenadiers organised a band of tribal irregulars for skirmishing and intelligence gathering in 1915. They patrolled the area of land between Sheikh Othman and the Turkish garrison in Lahej with great success, perhaps because they were more suited to the environment than the other Allied forces in the area. This irregular tribal band was regularised as the 1st Yemen Infantry in 1918, although partially raised in 1917 under the title of the Arab Legion. On Major M.C. Lake assuming command of the regiment, it was officially designated the 1st Yemen Infantry. While recruiting took place, there was an Arab Labour Corps, which was mainly composed of men from the hinterland, and had knowledge of the Turkish military occupation of their villages. They had come to Aden in the hopes of finding better conditions and more profitable work under the British flag. On the disbandment of the Labour Corps, some of the best men were selected for the 1st Yemen Infantry. At first, two companies

were recruited of approximately 400 men, and later increased to four companies, and finally reduced to three in 1922. Over 1,000 names appear on the medal roll for the British War and Victory medals. The unit was based at Sheikh Othman in the vacated Aden Troop accommodation. Colonel Meinhertzhagen inspected the force in 1923 and reported that their military value was nil. As a consequence of his report, the unit was disbanded in 1925.

Indian Officer, Aden Troop, 1911. Left of the Pugri was in light khaki with dark red stripes, right in light khaki with dark red folds, and green mullah (pointed skull cap). Tunic was in light khaki, and had steel shoulder chains with gilt rank pips, and deep yellow kurta. Shoes were black with solid overall gilt buckles, steel scabbard and hilt. Sword knot was in brown leather, alternatively dark green puttees and black boots with steel spurs, dark brown leather belts, gilt solid oblong waist belt plate, pouch belt with steel chains to edges and steel fittings, scarlet cummerbund, and gilt buttons. Gauntlets were in brown leather. (Thomas based on Lovett)

1st Yemen Infantry, Aden 1921 (David Birtles)

Officers and British NCOs of 1st Yemen Infantry ca 1920. The officer commanding, Captain M. Lake, appears in the second row, second from the left. The tall officer in the centre is Lt. Pearce, later captain Queen's Royal West Surrey Regiment. The RSM appears on the far left of the front row. (Bill Cranston)

UNIFORM

British officers and men wore a solar topee with a diamond flash on the left-hand side with the words YEMEN 1st INFANTRY, in white, in three tiers. Brass metal shoulder titles with the same words as the topee flash were also worn. Arab soldiers and officers wore their own distinctive khaki *pagri* with a plain coloured flash on the left-hand side. All ranks wore a khaki tunic and shorts, with a leather belt. Soldiers wore a leather bandolier, while officers wore a Sam Browne. All Arabs and British Warrant Officers and Senior Non-Commissioned Officers wore full-length puttees.

23 (FORTRESS) COMPANY, ROYAL BOMBAY SAPPERS AND MINERS

In 1900 the Bombay Sappers and Miners included a service company in Aden. It appears that this service company was replaced by a fortress company in 1902 as no further reference to it in Aden is mentioned in Sandes' *The Indian Sappers and Miners*. By 1903 the Fortress Company was renamed 23 (Fortress) Company, 3rd Sappers and Miners and was located in Aden. 23rd (Fortress) Company, Royal Bombay Sappers and Miners, as it became known in 1921, remained in Aden until disbanded in 1928.

45 (ADEN) RIFLES

An infantry unit known as the Aden Rifles was formed on 1 January 1917 by Army Department notification number 1588 of 1916. With an establishment of one reserve company, this unit was reconstituted as an Indian Defence Force unit, with the designation of 45 (Aden) Rifles from 1 April 1917. This volunteer force was raised from the local population and a small number of British officers, for the defence of Aden during the First World War. Officers of the Company were Major Harold Berridge OBE who raised the unit and was attached to the Royal Engineers (RE), Major James Bett Grey, who became the Commandant, Captain Henry Zoro Roycroft, Lt. Cyril Eric Leman, Lt. Stanley Nicholas Day, Lt. Thomas Williamson McLachlan, 2/Lt Eric Randal and Supernumerary Captain Edward Merle Duggan. With the general demobilisation and down-scaling of forces in the Indian Army, the company was disestablished in 1920. Although some sources indicate the unit existed until 1934, this was probably on paper only. The IDF became Auxiliary Force India in 1920.

Little is known about the Aden Rifles historically or about the badges and insignia worn. In recent years a few artifacts have surfaced and these include a fine caste, white metal, two tiered curved title 67 ADEN RIFLES, but to date the author can find no evidence of the unit ever being formed with that number. The solar topee flash had the words ADEN RIFLES in white on a black over red diagonally intersected rectangle. There is an unconfirmed report of an Aden Rifles headdress badge described as a delicate die cast, in the shape of a pear/tear drop, 40mm x 28mm. Within the 'outer perimeter', muskets, crossed halfway along the barrels their slings falling symmetrically behind a scroll across the butts – at about 30 degrees upwards on each side – inscribed ADEN RIFLES. Voided throughout, the badge is reputedly brass and has lugs. 410 Rifleman S.O. Whitley, 45th Aden Rifles, Indian Defence Force, was awarded Mentioned in Despatches (Aden Field Force GGO 1747, dated 27 August 1920). His MID was awarded for showing great coolness, courage and devotion to duty under fire when driving the steam roller during the construction of the Robat Road. Though under shell fire every day while at this work he never withdrew his roller out of range even when the machine was hit by shrapnel.

In 1904, Harold Berridge went to Aden as Chief Engineer to the Aden Port Trust, a position he retained until his retirement in 1924. In 1917 he was commissioned into the Indian Defence Force as a Major, and Commandant of 45th Aden Rifles. From 1918 to 1920 he served as Garrison Engineer and Deputy Assistant Director of Railways with the Aden Field Force. He was mentioned in despatches twice and appointed Companion of the Order of the Indian Empire (CIE) and Officer of the Order of the British Empire (OBE) in the 1919 Indian War Honours. He relinquished his commission in September 1920 but was permitted to retain his rank.

90 COMPANY ROYAL ARMY SERVICE CORPS/90 SQUADRON ROYAL CORPS OF TRANSPORT

Raised on 1 December 1957, in Aden, this unit was largely composed of locally enlisted staff. The role of the unit was to supply staff cars and administrative vehicles for Middle East Command and the various other units in the Aden garrison. The unit was retitled 90 Squadron RCT in 1965. With the run-down of British Troops in Aden due to the withdrawal the unit moved to Sharjah.

653 SQUADRON ARMY AIR CORPS

653 Squadron AAC provided aviation support British Troops in Aden during the Emergency. The squadron was initially equipped with nine fixed-wing Auster and Beaver aircraft and two Scout helicopters and provided air reconnaissance, resupply, liaison and artillery fire direction. By 1966, the squadron was retitled No. 3 Wing AAC, but still used the official crest of 653 Squadron. It comprised of No. 15 Flight AAC with seven DH-C 2 Beavers, No. 8 Flight AAC and No. 13 Flight AAC, each with six Westland Scout Helicopters and 4 or 5 'Air Troops' or 'Air

Army Air Corps de Haviland Beaver. WAP mid-1960s. (Tony Ford)

Platoons'. Each of these comprised of three Augusta/Westland Sioux-Bell 47G helicopters. A very effective Workshop was also a part of the unit. These came under command of 3 Wing AAC for all servicing and technical standards, but under the command of individual military combat units when required for service. 3 Wing AAC was based at Falaise Camp's airfield, near Little Aden, but for the last six months of 1967, moved to Khormaksar until the final withdrawal.

1401 (ADEN) COMPANY, PIONEER CORPS

In 1940, two Pioneer Corps companies were raised in Aden to provide labour for the Somaliland Campaign. Tasks involved road maintenance, airfield construction and port operation. Generally pioneer companies were of no fixed size, but usually were between 100 and 500 men. Although independent and self-sufficient, the companies were clustered into Groups for administrative purposes. Most foreign companies were unarmed.

On 2 November 1940 British staff arrived at Tawahi to raise 1401 (Aden) Company. By the end of January 1941, the total strength of locally recruited men was 574. Because of the good response to recruiting, the officer commanding, Major J.V.L. Kell of the South Staffordshire Regiment, decided to raise another company, 1402 (Aden) Company. Major Kell was then appointed to command the Group, which was responsible for 1401–1419 Companies. Major Kell was later replaced by Captain D.N. Seton of The Welch Regiment.

The company sailed from Aden on 14 March 1941. Troops disembarked from their transport at Berbera two days later in small boats. They formed up on the foreshore at the rear of the infantry, and then moved up to Berbera town in field formation. The sight of so many troops advancing on the town, even though the pioneers were unarmed, was enough for the Italian garrison to put up only minimal resistance before quickly decamping. Berbera was soon captured, and the company commenced construction of a road to the pier and provided working parties to unload lighters. After this successful campaign, the company returned to Aden on 16 April 1941, and disbanded on 21 May. The uniform was simply khaki shorts and shirts.

1402 (ADEN) COMPANY, PIONEER CORPS

The company was formed on 1 February 1941, from the surplus of 1401 Company, and was commanded by Captain S.H.J. Harrison, Royal Sussex Regiment. Initially 100 men were employed with the RAF at the aerodrome in Aden. On 14 March 1941 the unit embarked at Aden for Berbera, with one British officer, three British other ranks, one Arab officer and 185 Arab other ranks. Bombardment of the town of Berbera by the Aden Striking Force commenced at about 0435 hrs on 16 March. At daybreak the company remained on board the troop transport *Chakdina* to assist with unloading cargo which was required for the attack. Later, the company was employed in levelling ground for an aerodrome and also worked on the pier road and various other duties for the Engineers and Ordnance Corps. After this successful tour in Somaliland, the company returned to Aden on 14 April, and was disbanded there a week later.

1422 (SULTAN SALEH'S HADHRAMAUT) COMPANY, PIONEER CORPS

On 27 March 1943 Captain D.N. Seton, of The Welch Regiment, was instructed to form a new pioneer company in Aden. A number of British other ranks from the Aden Protectorate Levies were selected and posted to the unit. Two Arab subalterns also joined the force, which consisted of six sections of 25 men. On 17 July 1943, the company arrived by ship at the port of Mukalla in the Eastern Aden Protectorate, where the unit was employed on road construction. Once the work was completed, the unit returned to Aden on 3 December 1943. Three days later they embarked for the island of Socotra to relieve 2004 Company, where the company was involved with unloading petrol and road construction until the end of January 1944. It is believed that the unit was disbanded shortly after the work was completed.

ADEN AIR RAID PRECAUTIONS (ARP)

The ARP organisation existed in Aden during the Second World War. Members had their own ARP lapel badge with the title ADEN.

ADEN DEFENCE LIGHT SECTION, INDIAN SUBMARINE CORPS

In 1899, Major A.M. Stuart, RE, began developing a system of electric light defence for the Indian ports. As a consequence of his efforts a section consisting of one British officer, two Mechanists and six other ranks (RE), with four Indian mechanics, was authorised for the maintenance of the electric defence lights, telegraphs and telephones at Aden. Affiliation with the 3rd Bombay Sappers and Miners took place in 1910. In 1912 the Indian Submarine Corps was abolished and the units were known as Defence Light Sections. The Aden Defence Light Section was amalgamated into 23 (Fortress) Company in 1927, and 23 (Fortress) Company. which was disbanded in 1928.

ADEN HOME GUARD

The Aden Home Guard was in existence from 1942 to 1944, with non-European as well as European companies. Three discarded RAF armoured cars were reconditioned by the Civil Government for the Home Guard.

ADEN LABOUR CORPS

A shortage of labour within the Colony and Protectorate gave rise to the establishment of the Aden Labour Corps during the Second World War. The units raised were the Aden Pioneer Corps, 1422 Hadhramaut Pioneer Company, 1401 and 1402 Aden Pioneer Companies. The Aden Labour Corps Ordinance 1940 was amended so that part of the Corps could serve outside the Colony. During 1940 the Corps came under the Air Ministry but later in 1940 the Army took responsibility.

The Corps consisted of the following ranks:

Commandant and British officers
Mulazim
Havildar
Mukaddam
Assistant Mukaddam
Private or Enlisted Follower

Uniform; pair khaki shorts, khaki shirt, one *aqu'al*, one *imama*.

ADEN ORDNANCE DEPOT

There was an Indian Army Ordnance Depot in Aden which separated from the Indian Army in 1928 and returned to the Indian Army in 1941.

ADEN POLICE

SHURTAT ADN

Troops of Aden Police existed as early as 1857. By 1928 the Aden Police were under the control of a Deputy Superintendent of the Bombay Provincial Police Department. Their task was conventional policing within the metropolitan area of Aden. The existence of one British and one Indian infantry battalion was of sufficient moral effect to prevent any trouble, as the battalions could be used to support the Aden Police.

With the change of responsibility for defence from Army to RAF, both battalions of infantry were removed, which consequently necessitated an improvement in the organisation of the existing police force. In addition, the police force needed to be brought up to strength, as well requiring a certain amount of reorganisation. It was soon realised that a force of armed police was necessary to furnish the moral support previously provided by the army battalions. Accordingly, the Government of India and the Government of Bombay tasked two police officers from the Indian Police Service to proceed to Aden, study the reorganisation of the Civil Police, and examine the scheme for the recruitment

Aden Armed Police marching with fixed bayonets ca 1937. Note the Indian influence with the style of headdress. Aden was a dependency of the Indian Government until 1937, when it became a Crown Colony. (David Birtles)

Aden Armed Police ca 1937 with AP Monogram on *pagri*. Belt buckle has ADEN ARMED POLICE and the man's number. ADEN ARMED is curved and below is the policeman's number and a straight POLICE below that. (Michael Preveser)

The Interim Police came into being on 9 January 1929, followed by the recruitment and training of the Permanent Armed Police, and the reorganisation of the Civil Police. The Superintendent of Police was a British officer of the Indian Police Service. He had sole charge of the Aden Police Force, Armed and Unarmed, and control of the detachment of the Armed Police in Perim Island and the Kamaran Islands. His uniform was that of the Indian Police. Accommodation for the interim force was at the infantry barracks in Crater, Aden. The interim force proved its worth and lasted until December 1931. That same year the newly formed Armed Police replaced the Aden Protectorate Levies platoon at Kamaran. There were disturbances in Crater between Arabs and Jews in 1932 which lasted several days, and the Armed Police were called out to patrol the streets, and to restore law and order.

When Aden became a Crown Colony in 1937, the Aden Police retained responsibility for the Colony and the islands of Perim and Kamaran. The Colonial Reports' Annual of 1938 lists the following Unarmed Police:

232 Aden Land and Sheikh Othman Foot Police
12 Perim Land Police
13 Sheikh Othman Mounted Police
62 Aden Harbour Police

In Aden there were 141 Armed Police, in addition to 33 on Perim Island, and 31 at Kamaran.

The Armed Police also provided military guards at Government House and manned roadblocks when necessary. They were armed with .303 Lee-Enfield rifles, and in later years, 9mm Sterling sub-machine guns. During the Second World War, a Temporary Additional Constabulary was added to the service. The Aden Armed Police was on 3 February 1942 proclaimed to be a Military Force under Section 34 of the Police Ordinance, 1937. They remained a Military Force until 10 October 1945 when the order was revoked. After the war the Civil Police grew in size and included the following sections: Uniformed Police Section; Traffic Section; Marine Police Section; Prison Department; Criminal Investigation Department; Special Branch; Police Band; Fire Brigade. The Aden Police became a part of the South Arabian Police on 1 June 1967.

The uniform issue for the Police during the 1930s was as follows:

one pair of putties
two pairs shorts
two shirts
one pair *chaplis*
one monogram A.P.
one Fez cap
one baton with hook
one whistle
one belt and buckle plate

The Armed Police were also issued with black boots.
Later that decade the uniform was to change and included:

one *kullah*
one *pagri*
two shirts
two pairs shorts
one pair putties

of armed police. Reports submitted in July 1928 recommended that the force should be organised as a whole under a District Superintendent of Police and an Assistant Superintendent. This would replace the Assistant Resident in charge of the Police, and the Deputy Superintendent in immediate charge. The majority of the proposals were accepted, and the establishment was set at two British officers, 14 inspectors, four *Jamadars* (a rank which may be described as the Indian equivalent of Assistant Sub-Inspector), 200 Armed Police, 292 constables and 13 clerks.

The Government of India regarded the local recruitment of the Armed Police as an experiment. Pending their local recruitment and training it was decided to employ an interim force of 115 Armed Police recruited from India, and men from the earlier disbanded Aden Troop. This force was not to be withdrawn until it was clear that the locally raised Armed Police were fully efficient and capable of carrying out the duties entrusted to them.

Aden Armed Police on Parade at Crater Barracks, Aden 1965. The officer taking the salute wears a khaki uniform and black peaked cap and shoes. Socks are khaki with blue turnovers. Leading the parade is an Arab officer wearing red ceremonial *pagri*, and blue hosetops with red turnover. The rank-and-file wear blue hosetops and *tarbooshes*. The entire parade wears khaki tunics and shorts, and black shoes and black leather belt with police buckle. (F.W. Bird)

one pair *chaplis*
one *durrie*

Equipment consisted of:

one water bottle with carrier
one haversack
one belt
one buckle plate
one bandolier leather
one pouch
one frog

From 1938 gazetted officers wore their uniform based on the Dress Regulations for Colonial Police Service (CPS) dated May 1938. The Aden Police hat badge was worn on the police cap, and on the front of the Wolseley-pattern helmet under a dark blue silk 8-fold *puggaree*. Collar badges, which depicted the badge of the colony on a shield, were worn on the full-dress and undress tunic collar. Mess dress collar badges were of sterling silver. Those badges worn on a khaki collar had a dark blue background of Melton cloth cut to the shape of the badge. All metal buttons were CPS pattern, *viz.* the Imperial Crown and a wreath surrounding the monogram CPS and embodying the motto SALUS POPULI. Buttons came in

Aden Armed Police in ceremonial dress on guard at Government House, Aden, 1952. (Hugh Walker)

Aden Police constable, Khormaksar 1957. He wears blue hosetops and *chaplis* without socks. Note the dark blue lanyard over his left shoulder. (David Birtles)

four sizes, and were chromium plated on nickel silver, except for those for mess dress, which were of silver.

The cap badge of the Police Force was the badge of the colony in white metal, encircled with the inscription ADEN POLICE in English and ADN in Arabic. The whole was surmounted by the Tudor Crown, which was replaced with the St Edward's Crown after 1953. An officer's-quality badge was issued after 1953, which was similar to the existing badge, but with the addition of blue enamel. At the same time new collar badges – which were a smaller version of the cap badge – were introduced. They were issued in white metal, voided white metal and silver. Chrome buttons with the force device were also worn after 1953.

Other ranks wore white metal titles with the letters AP on the epaulettes of their shirts. Each policeman's number was stamped on the white metal clasp of his leather belt. The clasp had the words ADEN POLICE above the crown and the number below the crown.

By 1967 the uniform of the Civil Police consisted of: khaki drill uniform with a blue *tarboosh*, blue hosetops, putties and black boots. Marine Police wore a white shirt and shorts, with the blue *tarboosh*. Traffic Police wore a khaki drill uniform with white sleeves, a blue peaked cap with a white cover, and blue hose tops and boots. The Fire Brigade wore a blue drill uniform of trousers, a jacket with a double row of buttons, and a blue cap. NCOs and constables had leather belts with large white metal buckles.

For ceremonial occasions Armed Police wore a khaki drill uniform with a red Punjabi-style *pagri* with a *shamla*. A red cummerbund, and red hosetops with puttees and black boots were also worn. Working dress consisted of a khaki drill uniform with a blue beret, blue hosetops, puttees and black boots.

Immediately after the departure of the British from Aden the cap badge was modified by the simple expedient of cutting the crown from the top of the badge.

ADEN PROTECTORATE LEVIES

JAISH MAHMIYYAT ADN

A squadron of RAF bombers arrived at Khormaksar airfield located just outside Aden in 1928. They were the tangible result of a decision made in April 1927 when Aden became an Air Command. The doctrine of Air Control would remain in force for the next 30 years.

Prior to 1928, the garrison in Aden consisted mainly of a small number Sappers and Miners, Royal Artillery, one British and one Indian infantry battalion. However, by 1927 trouble was stirring in the Western Aden Protectorate. It was estimated that a divisional-sized military force was required to contain the problem, and

Officers of the Aden Protectorate Levies in 1932. Left to right, front row: RSM, unknown, Senior RAF officer, Lt. Col. Robinson DSO., Col. M.C. Lake, Capt. E. Hamilton, Ahmad Salih Maqtaria; back row: D.J. Hassama, Dr. Bashiri, Salim Islam Azzani, Hanash Ahmed Aulaqi, Capt. Fazal Ahmed BEM., Al Khader Mohsin Aulaqi. (Lt. Col. Nadir Ali, MBE)

APL Camel Troop ca 1937. The officers' headdress is a solar topee. The Levies wear their distinctive *mashedda* and *khulla*. All have a green flash on their headdress with white horizontal bar and green fringe. (David Birtles)

APL man a 40mm Bofors quick-firing AA gun during the Second World War. (British Crown Copyright/MOD)

APL camel mortar section ca 1950. The weapon is a British 3-inch mortar Mk.III. (British Crown Copyright/MOD)

APL *jundies* show off the various orders of dress ca 1950. The khaki shirt has no collar and only one pocket on the left-hand side. The sandals are locally made (British Crown Copyright/MOD)

APL Quarter Guard at Lodar, WAP, 1958. (Tom Wylie)

it was successfully argued that air power could do the job for a fraction of the price. This innovative idea worked well in the short term. To secure the airfields a body of men was raised on 1 April 1928. Known as the Aden Protectorate Levies (APL), they were also available to assist the Civil Police when required.

The APL were recruited mainly from the Western Aden Protectorate tribes. Colonel M.C. Lake, of the Indian Army, became the first commanding officer of a unit which consisted of two British officers and six platoons of Arab infantry. The Arab officers held governor's commissions. The unit had eight mules and 48 camels on its strength. Since Aden was administered by the Bombay Presidency until 1937, it was more strongly influenced by New Delhi than London. For example, the APL had a strong Indian Army stamp on it. A number of senior NCOs and junior officers were Indian. Even the headdress was a Punjabi-style turban or *pagri*, rather than the traditional Arab *imama*. Having set up the Levies, Colonel Lake handed over command in 1929 to Lieutenant Colonel J.C. Robinson DSO, who remained in command for 10 years. One of the platoons was converted to a Machine Gun Camel Troop, which became mechanised in 1938.

To provide cover from air attack, an anti-aircraft Wing was formed by 1939, and during the Second World War an Italian plane was shot down. During the war the strength of the Levies increased from 600 to 1,600 men, and they provided garrisons in Socotra Island and Sharjah, in addition to their other duties in the Western Aden Protectorate and Aden Colony. Establishment increases in 1942 provided for RHQ, Headquarters Company, training company, anti-aircraft battery, signal Company and 10 rifle companies. In April 1943 the garrison at Socotra was increased to three companies, and two 75mm field guns for anti-submarine defence were added. By 1946 the complement of the Levies had risen to over 1,800 men.

By 1948, Royal Air Force Regiment officers and airmen had replaced army personnel, a process which had started as early as 1942. As a consequence of this new policy, the APL became organised as a tactical force of two Wings, each about the size of an infantry battalion, and an administration Wing. This later became three Wings, each of three infantry squadrons. From 1947 onwards, there was much turmoil within the Western Aden Protectorate, and the Levies were frequently in action. The APL duties in 1953 were Aid to the Civil Power. Internal security roles were allotted and exercised.

MASIRAH DETACHMENT
There was a permanent commitment to keep a Flight on the Island of Masirah.

ADEN GUARDS.
A guard was provided for the ordnance depot in Jebel Haddid at night.

CAMEL TROOP

Camel Troop was only used for ceremonial purposes. Local camels were hired when required for operations.

The APL did not have air support communications in the early 1950s. If required, it was necessary to take along an Air Controller who had his own VHF radio for communicating with the aircraft including Vampires and Shackleton Mk.2 Bombers. The

An RAF Regiment weapons instructor pointing out the finer skills on the .303 Mk II Bren Gun to a *jundi* in the late 1940s or early 1950s. The RAF Regiment instructor wears a bush hat with the left-hand brim turned up. A locally manufactured crossed *jambia* badge is pinned onto a green APL flash with a vertical white line superimposed. (British Crown Copyright/MOD)

An Arab APL officer in the 1950s. The all-khaki uniform bears a green lanyard and garter flashes. The RAF style rank insignia is green and white. The headdress reflects the Indian influence of earlier years. The *mashedda* headdress is khaki and has a *khulla* on top. On the left-hand side of the headdress is a green flash with fringe and a white horizontal bar. (British Crown Copyright/MOD)

APL bugler ca 1951. The green and white Levies headdress flash and fringe is clearly seen. The leather bugle cords are green. (British Crown Copyright/MOD)

Profile of an Arab APL officer showing parade uniform in the 1950s. (British Crown Copyright/MOD)

bombers would make a stately run, dropping bombs and firing machine guns as well. In theory, casualty evacuation by air could be provided by RAF Sycamore helicopters. Mukeiras and Dhala camps were often shot-up at night, as were resupply convoys for the Government Guard fort at Marta'a (Merta). In 1954 an APL convoy sent to relieve a remote fort was ambushed in the Wadi Hatib and suffered many casualties. In 1957 administration of the Levies changed when the War Office assumed control. RAF personnel moved out and were replaced by British Army officers and a fourth battalion of infantry was formed. With headquarters at Seedaseer Lines, Khormaksar, there were 'up-country' bases at Dhala, Mukeiras, Beihan and occasional outstations at Zinjibar, Lodar and Ataq. In 1958 the Levies, supported by the Shropshire Light Infantry and the RAF, fought off a strong force of Yemeni troops and dissident tribesmen on the Jebel Jihaf, driving them back over the Yemen border. During the late 1950s, operations focused on border hostilities with the Yemen, and were similar in style to operations on the Indian Frontier. Good picquetting drill was essential for survival. The Yemenis often crossed the border for 'shoot-up raids', a murder or just cattle rustling.

By the end of the decade support and ancillary units included a very capable signal squadron, a RAF-run hospital, an Armoured Car Squadron equipped with Ferret Scout Cars, a Royal Artillery battery and a Training Battalion of the APL. A Camel Company was retained, and later called the Camel Flight, which was eventually used for ceremonial occasions only. Discipline in the APL was generally good, but there was a tendency for desertion or going absent without leave, because a man's real loyalty was to his tribe, village, family or clan. If he was not able to get leave whenever required then he would take so-called 'French leave' so as to play his part in the family, tribal disputes or harvesting, after which he would return to his military duty. The soldier was armed with a Rifle, No. 4 Mk I, which he was permitted to keep when discharged. A modern rifle, in a country where the rifle was the mark of a man, was indeed worth soldiering for. With the creation of the Federation of Amirate of the South, the Aden Protectorate Levies were eventually renamed the Federal Regular Army on 30 November 1961 and changed their allegiance from Queen Elizabeth to the Federation.

ARMOURED CARS

Two Rolls Royce Armoured Cars from the Armoured Car Wing Iraq were sent to D Flight No. 8 Squadron RAF in Aden on 13 January 1928. The RAF Armoured Car Section was first established in Aden in 1929 and comprised two Rolls Royce Armoured Cars, one Crossley six-wheeler and a total of 23 all ranks. A list of vehicles used in Aden up until 1950 is as follows:

The Annual Colonial Reports for 1937 show that there was a Section of Armoured Cars stationed at Tawahi (Steamer Point) which belonged to the RAF. The Aden Armoured Car Section handed over three Crossley six-wheeler armoured cars, and one Rolls Royce Armoured Car, in August 1939 to the 2/5th Mahratta Light Infantry. The section was equipped at that time with Alvis Armoured Cars.

Table 5: Aden Armoured Car Section & 4001 Flight Armoured Fighting Vehicles Establishment 1928–1950

13 January 1928	2 Rolls Royce Armoured Cars from Armoured Car Wing, Iraq 'D' Flight, No. 8 Squadron RAF
29 January 1929	Aden Section Armoured Cars formed: 2 Rolls Royce Armoured Cars, 1 Crossley six-wheeler (W/T & R/T, 2 Officers, 1 Sergeant, 3 Corporals, 17 Airmen)
14 December 1932	Crossley six-wheeler No. 50401 arrived from Iraq
1 November 1937	One Rolls Royce Armoured Car arrived from Iraq (total 3 Rolls Royce Armoured Cars and 2 Crossley six-wheelers)
29 November 1938	Section re-equipped with four Alvis Armoured Cars
19 January 1939	Rolls Royce Armoured Cars not being used. (Total: 4 Alvis Armoured Cars and 3 Crossley Armoured Cars)
25 August 1939	3 Crossleys and 1 Rolls Royce Armoured Cars handed over to 2/5 Mahratta Light Infantry
3 September 1939	Establishment at declaration of War: 2 officers, 1 Sergeant, 18 Airmen, 4 Alvis Armoured Cars
28 August 1940	2 Fordson Armoured Cars and 4 Alvis Armoured Cars
31 August 1940	4 Alvis Armoured Cars shipped to UK (total: 2 Fordson Armoured Cars)
08 March 1943	2 Fordson Armoured Cars (RAF 301 and RAF 304)
25 April 1944	(Total: 3 GMC Light Armoured Recce Cars 226, 229,300)
07 December 1944	GMCs named RAF226 'HMAC Cavalier', RAF300 'HMAC Chieftain'
30 April 1945	GMCs renumbered with 555 added e.g. 555226
01 November 1945	GMCs handed over to APL
05 November 1945	Humber Armoured Cars collected: 920, 921, 922 (Mk IV)
03 October 1946	Renamed 4001 Armoured Car Flight
04 September 1946	Humbers known as Able, Baker and Charlie. Later 5 Humbers and 1 Daimler
1947	Humbers replaced by GMCs. GMC Recce Cars 807, 814, 822, 837 and 541. The Flight is redesignated 4001 Armoured Car Flight, RAF Regiment
1948	(Total: 7 GMCs)
06 August 1950	Flight departs for Amman

RAF Fordson armoured car and Ford 15 CWT CMP 4x4 in Aden during the 1930s or 1940s. (British Crown Copyright/MOD)

Canadian GM Otter Light Recce Car, ca later 1940s. (British Crown Copyright/MOD)

The Aden Armoured Car Section became known as 4001 Armoured Car Flight, RAF Regt. in 1947. No. 4001 Armoured Car Flight, Aden, moved to Amman, Jordan in August 1950.

During 1956, 10 Armoured Car Squadron APL was raised and issued with Ferret Mk 2 Scout Cars. The crew was entirely RAF personnel. On 1 April 1957, the APL transferred to the British Army with the RAF personnel being replaced gradually by British Army crew. The squadron consisted of four Sabre Troops and a Headquarters:

SHQ
A Flight later known as 1 Troop when under Army control
B Flight later known as 2 Troop when under Army control
C Flight later known as 3 Troop when under Army control
D Flight later known as 4 Troop when under Army control

Squadron personnel gradually became all-Arab with 3 Troop being the first all-Arab Troop under the command of Troop Leader Mulazim Mohamed Hamed Yaffi. Saladin Armoured Cars were introduced circa 1966–1967. Members of 10 Squadron APL prior to the Army control wore the insignia of crossed *jambias* over a green cloth disk which was worn on a RAF beret. This was not an authorised badge but a locally made emblem which was accepted within the command.

HOSPITAL
A hospital for the Levies had been established before the 1950s along with a medical Wing. (See RAF Section)

WEAPONS
APL weapons used in 1953–1954 included:

.303 Rifle No. 4 Mk I
2-inch Mortar (each Flight had a 2-inch mortar section)
Sten Gun (officers and SNCOs carried Sten Guns or revolvers as personal weapons)
3-inch Mortar (one per Flight)

Vickers Medium Machine Guns were also used in more static environments

UNIFORM
During the 1950s, when 'up-country' the uniform of the Arab APL troops consisted of khaki drill shirts and shorts, grey woollen socks rolled down to the ankles, and brown (blue when under the RAF) canvas shoes (plimsolls). The headdress was a simple roll of khaki cloth, worn over the head in a style known as a *mashedda* or Audhali turban. The name comes from the type of headdress worn by the Audhali tribe, which provided much of the manpower for the APL. All ranks would wear the *mashedda* up-country so officers could not be seen at a distance by enemy snipers. British soldiers had a similar

RAF GMC Otter Armoured car of 4001 Flight in Aden. Late 1940s. (Sean Brady)

Table 6: Comparative Ranks

APL pre-1957	Post-1957	British equivalent rank
	Zaim	Brigadier
	Aqid	Colonel
	Qaid	Lieutenant Colonel
Bimbashi al Awal	Wakil Qaid	Major
Bimbashi	Rais	Captain
Yuzbashi	Mulazim Awal	Lieutenant
Mulazim	Mulazim Thani	2nd Lieutenant
Sergeant Major	Wakil Dabit Awal	Regimental Sergeant Major
	Wakil Dabit I Imdadat	Regimental Quartermaster Sergeant
	Naqib As Sariya	Company Sergeant Major
Bash Shawoosh	Naib Awal	Staff Sergeant
Shawoosh	Naib	Sergeant
Wakil	Areef	Corporal
Naib Wakil	Wakil Areef	Lance Corporal
Askar	Jundi	Private

scroll with APL and the whole surmounted by the crown of Queen Elizabeth. An anodized aluminium badge with the same design was later issued. Brass APL shoulder titles were worn, although some troops wore unofficial white-on-green cloth titles with the name of their unit spelled out in full. Coloured battalion lanyards were introduced when the APL became an Army responsibility:

HQ – green and white twist
1st Battalion – orange
2nd Battalion – blue
3rd Battalion – red
4th Battalion – Cambridge blue
Support squadrons wore the lanyard of the corresponding Corps in the British Army. Prior to that the RAF-controlled APL wore a green lanyard.

up-country uniform, except that they wore khaki drill slacks and suede desert boots, and often wore locally made ammunition belts of soft leather instead of the cotton bandoleers. These locally made belts had 55 loops for individual bullets, and a carrying strap for the *jambia*, which was the preferred equipment of the Arab soldier. The informality of the uniform up-country helped identify British personnel as belonging to the APL rather than to the British Army.

Ceremonial dress was worn by members of the Camel Troop, Camp Police and the Guard of Honour. This uniform consisted of a khaki or white drill bush jacket and shorts, black boots and khaki short puttees with green hosetops and green and white garter tabs. An elaborate Punjabi-style white *pagri*, with a *shamla*, was worn with a red stripe on the front, and a green flash with a white bar on the left-hand side. A khaki *pagri* was the normal parade headdress. During the late 1940s to early 1950s the British instructors wore a slouch hat with an APL flash of horizontal green–white–green, superimposed on which was a locally made cap badge of metal crossed *jambias*. Army officers wore the British officers' service dress cap. Until the early 1950s RAF officers were issued with Bombay bowlers, a khaki helmet similar to a polo helmet. The unofficial APL badge was worn over a green backing cut out to the shape of the badge. RAF personnel were issued with the RAF blue beret on which they wore the unofficial APL badge on a green cloth disk. Army personnel, who replaced the RAF in 1957, sometimes wore an APL 'Cap, Field Service' aka side cap, British army-style, of green with white piping. Walking out dress in the 1950s consisted of a white *mashedda*, and a white shirt with a green cloth diamond over the left breast pocket, and khaki shorts.

Queen Elizabeth II authorised the badge of the APL on 11 December 1955. Its description is 'Two *jambias* points downwards in saltire enfiled by a circlet. Motto 'Peace be with you' in Arabic'. The significance of the *jambias* was that they are weapons carried by all tribesmen in Aden and are unique to them. The circlet of the traditional green colour of the unit suggests unity of the various formations of Levies. Locally made badges were worn until about 1958, when the army introduced an official APL cap badge, initially in brass and white metal or silver and gilt for officers. This badge was similar to the previous badge except that it now had a

Non-uniformed civilian personnel on the strength of the APL included medical officers, clerks who also acted as interpreters, cooks and medical orderlies, syces for the horses, mess staff, officers' bearers and sweepers.

While under RAF command technicians wore inverted chevrons, and this did not change immediately after reverting to Army control.

ADEN SIGNAL COMPANY, BOMBAY SAPPERS AND MINERS

In September 1915 a Sub-Inspector with three operators and six linemen arrived from India tasked with providing communications for the Aden Movable Column, in addition to the regimental signallers of the infantry units. It was originally thought that communications were needed for two brigades, however a decision was made to downgrade the theatre of operations and Lahej was allowed to remain in the hands of the Turkish Army. On 26 March 1917 the detachment officially became the Aden Signal Company. The unit included a Brigade Signal Section, Divisional HQ Section with two Heavy Cable Sections, Motorcycle Section, Artillery Section and a Line of Communications Section. The following year a wireless detachment was added. After hostilities ceased the company was redesignated Aden Brigade Signal Section, and in 1922 became the Aden Signal Section. This Indian Signal Corps unit became a Royal Signals unit in 1927.

ADEN SUPPLY DEPOT (201)

The Bombay Commissariat maintained a Supply Depot from 1862 in Aden which came under the Supply and Transport Corps in 1901, which in turn was renamed the Indian Army Service Corps in 1923. In 1935 the corps was granted the 'Royal' prefix and became known as Royal Indian Army Service Corps (RIASC). The Depot consisted of several sections. 201 Supply Depot Aden consisted of several sections all numbered 201. In 1943 it was renamed Aden Supply Depot and in 1947 it was taken over by the British Royal Army Service Corps.

ADEN TRANSPORT COMPANY

The Aden Transport Company existed from 1923 to 1928 and consisted of 120 camels, pack and draught. The Supply & Transport establishment was under an Assistant Director Supply & Transport (Colonel Thacker) who was assisted by two British warrant officers. Aden Mechanical Transport Section was also included in the ATC. This Indian Army Service Corps unit separated from the Indian Army in 1928.

ADEN TROOP

On 16 November 1855 a troop of irregular horse was sanctioned for Aden. The officer appointed to command the troop sailed from India on 20 April 1856, however the ship returned to India. Although 13 horses and two ponies were indented for on 3 March 1857, the irregular horse never arrived. Instead, the officer volunteered his troop for the Persian War, after which it went to India to serve against the Mutineers.

A Colonel Merewether finally raised a troop of cavalry in Aden in 1867–68 and named it the Aden Levy. Recruitment for the troop was made in Baluchistan (India), with volunteers coming from the Poona Horse and the 1st and 2nd Scinde Horse. The Levy was regularised as the Aden Troop, a sub-unit of the Indian Army. Indian Army officers were seconded to the troop, and by 1875 the unit's furthest outpost was at Khormaksar, on the isthmus of sand which linked Aden to the mainland.

In 1881, the Kotaibi tribe from the Radfan Mountains commenced exacting dues on the Hardaba route. This ancient, but illegal, form of revenue collection was dealt with in July 1884 when it was found necessary to support the Amir of Dhala with 50 sabres of Aden Troop and some sappers. Following the destruction of a few forts the Kotaibi quickly gave in. The following year the troop revisited the area to deter Turkish encroachment. This had little effect as in the summer of 1886 the Turks established themselves near Jalela and built a fortified post. Aden Troop consisted of 100 troopers in 1897 including 45 being camel *sowars*. During 1900–1901, Aden Troop participated in operations in Jubaland, and between 1902 and 1904, acted as escort to the Anglo-Turkish Boundary Commission. A highlight of the troop's existence was the Imperial Visit to India in 1911, during which it provided the King's escort in Aden. The troop was lined up four-deep, with horses and camels mounted by bearded, khaki-clad troopers. In 1915, the troop formed the advance guard during the British march to Lahej, a move aimed at preventing a Turkish advance upon Aden. The troop was disbanded in 1927, but a number of the troopers were later to see service with the newly formed Aden Protectorate Levies and the Aden Armed Police. The Marquis of Cambridge in his 'Notes on the Armies of India' in the Journal of the Society for Army Historical Research mentions the Aden Troop, and giving their battle honours as Persia, Indian Mutiny, Somaliland 1890 and Aden 1901.

During the 60 years of its existence the uniform of the Aden Troop would have undergone numerous changes, although information on dress is sketchy at best. One source states that in 1897 their uniform was dark green with yellow facings and a yellow throat plume on the bridle. In his book *Forces of the British Empire 1914*, Nevins indicates that the uniform included a khaki turban, *kurta*, cummerbund and breeches with khaki puttees. Indian Army ranks were used. The parade dress at the time of the Imperial visit was typical of an Indian cavalry regiment. A metal shoulder title is reputed to have been worn consisting of crossed lances with pennants surmounted by a crown. The monogram AT superimposed on the crossed lances in the centre.

COUNTER INTELLIGENCE COMPANY ADEN

From 1956, members of the Intelligence Corps were sent to Aden to provide intelligence support for British and APL/FRA/SAA units. Some Corps members were in staff appointments while the others were in 4 Field Security Section (FSS) from 1957. During the 1964 Radfan Operation, Corps members who were mainly from 15 Intelligence Platoon supported 39 Brigade. Some officers worked for Joint Staff Intelligence (Middle East), HQ, MELF, HQ 24 Brigade and HQ Aden Brigade. Counter Intelligence Company Aden evolved from 4 FSS to provide security expertise. The CIC was involved with interrogation at Fort Morbut Holding Centre for the collation of intelligence and house raids with Special Branch.

DESERT GUARDS

HARAS AL SAHARA

Desert Guards were auxiliaries of the Hadhrami Bedouin Legion and consisted of local tribesmen who were attached to HBL posts. The tribesmen found their own weapons and rations and were paid a monthly wage. Although ammunition was provided, they were expected to account for it. Some attempts were made to drill the tribesmen, although their principal value lay in their contacts with, and intelligence gathered from, local tribes. Nevertheless, they did take part in many desert skirmishes. Where supplied, uniforms consisted of HBL khaki *qamees* and a green chequered *imama* with black *aqu'al*.

FEDERAL NATIONAL GUARD

HARAS AL ITTIHAD

With the creation of the Federation of the Amirates of the South in 1959, the Government Guards and Tribal Guard were renamed the Federal National Guard (FNG). They became known as FNG1 and FNG2 respectively and were placed under Federal control. The new force continued to operate in the former Western Aden Protectorate as an armed gendarmerie, serving in lieu of a police force.

FNG1 was recruited from all the States of the Federation and was directly controlled from the Federal National Guard Headquarters at Champion Lines in Aden. By contrast, FNG2 consisted of former Tribal Guard or State forces, recruited entirely from within their own States. FNG2 units were chiefly officered by relations and friends of the various State rulers. Although FNG2 contingents were administered from FNG Headquarters, in practice they conformed to the wishes of the State Rulers in most matters. The Commander FNG never managed to get FNG2 solely under his control because the State rulers, who collectively formed the Federal Council, always objected to losing personal control of their own forces.

Unlike the Federal Regular Army (FRA), the FNG received no support or advice from the British Army. Although the FNG commander was British, almost all of the officers were Arab. One consequence of the different organisational structures was the considerable rivalry between the two forces. As the insurgency problem in the federation increased, so too did the pressure on the FNG There was general dissatisfaction on the British side regarding the FNG's standard and performance.

During the summer of 1965 a reorganisation of the FNG took place, which included retraining and reequipping thus rendering it better able to play a part in responding to the insurgency problem. FNG1 was reorganised into four *katibas*, which were similar to infantry battalions. A committee was formed to advise on the future pattern of the Federal forces, and it was decided that the four *katibas* of FNG1 should be absorbed into the FRA to form the South Arabian Army (SAA), while FNG2 should be expanded and join the existing Aden Police to form the new South Arabian Police (SAP). During this period, the Federal Government was informed by HM Government that all British forces were to be pulled out of Aden, and that British military support to the Federal forces would cease. This reduced the authority of the State Rulers and the Federal Council. The two terrorist organisations, National Liberation Front (NLF) and the Front for the Liberation of the South Yemen (FLOSY) were greatly encouraged and were able to step up their operations against the Federal Government to a considerable degree. The Federal forces came under great political pressure to support the terrorist organisations. While still being paid by the Federation, many members were secretly establishing links with the NLF, which soon established itself as the dominant terrorist force. In 1967, the four *katibas* of FNG1 joined the FRA to form the South Arabian Army, but before the expansion and reorganisation of the new South Arabian Police could be completed the final storm broke. Terrorist pressure intensified and revolutions took place in one State after another. In the last few months of the Federation, all of the State rulers disappeared over the border, the Federal Council ceased to operate, and the Minister of Internal Security left the country. As most of the officers of FNG2 were closely connected to the State rulers, most of them fled as well, thereby rendering adequate control of FNG2 impossible.

UNIFORM

Working dress for the Federal National Guard consisted of a khaki shirt, shorts, black hose tops with khaki puttees and boots. On occasion, khaki or green overalls were also worn by other ranks. Three types of head dress were worn. Officers wore a black *sedara*, or field service cap, with a green crown and green piping, on the front of which was placed a small-sized white metal FNG cap badge. Other ranks were issued with a khaki beret, or a black *pagri*, on both of which were worn brass badges. The ceremonial *pagri* had a black tail which hung down below the back of the neck. Black buttons, which bore the FNG insignia, were worn by all ranks, and came in two sizes. A black lanyard was worn on the left shoulder. Officers wore green cloth Arabic shoulder titles sewn to the tops of their tunic sleeves, and highly decorated, locally made, black cartridge belts together with a black Sam Browne belt. Arabic white metal shoulder titles were worn on some orders of dress, while those for other ranks were brass. Green cummerbunds were worn on ceremonial occasions. Embellishments on the other ranks' khaki cloth tunic included khaki cloth shoulder titles with black Arabic script. Other ranks leather equipment consisted of black belts, ammunition pouches and straps. British rank insignia was worn by all ranks.

Cap badges were made in white metal for officers and brass for other ranks. The Arabic motto on the cap badge translates as 'God commands justice, the doing of good'. Other insignia included khaki drill square patches with black numbers ranging from 1 to 24. Patterns for these patches were sealed on 7 November 1960. Tribal insignia was also authorised and consisted of a khaki square with the name of the State in black Arabic lettering. Patterns for the tribal insignia, which was almost certainly used by FNG2, were sealed on 10 February 1961. Black and silver buttons were issued, both of which bore the design of the cap badge. Small white metal collar badges, in mirrored pairs, were produced for officers.

Brigadier J.H. Mallard, last commandant of the FNG. He has a black lanyard and an Arabic style *sedara* headdress with a silver, officers' pattern cap badge. (Brigadier Mallard)

FNG bugler. Note the black headdress with tail hang down the neck. (Bill Cranston)

Ferret Scout Car of the FRA Armoured Car Squadron in Wadi Said, 1967. (Peter Herrett)

Vickers Machine Gun Crew. The GPMG 7.62 mm machine gun was offered as a replacement during a force re-equipment program in 1967 but was refused. (David Birtles)

FEDERAL REGULAR ARMY

JAISH AL ITTIHAD AL NIDHAMI

The APL had formed part of the Imperial Forces, but once handed over to the Federal Government as the Federal Regular Army (FRA) on 30 November 1961, it owed allegiance to Aden, not London. The General Officer Commanding Middle East Land Forces (MELF) continued to have some residual responsibilities for the FRA until 1 April 1964 after which date the Federal Government had complete control. At the end of 1961 the strength of the FRA was about 4,500 officers and men including about 400 seconded British personnel.

When formed, the FRA consisted of four infantry battalions, a training battalion, an armoured car squadron, a signal squadron, a motor transport company, a supply platoon and a force workshop. A British artillery battery supported the force. A fifth battalion was raised in 1964. Each battalion comprised three rifle companies, a headquarters company containing a Vickers Medium Machine Gun platoon and a 3-inch mortar platoon. The training battalion, located at Sheikh Othman, was virtually a depot and also administered the ceremonial Camel Troop, which was 16-camels-strong being all that was remained of the old APL Camel Company. Other subunits included the apprentices' school and force band, which were included in the depot's strength.

FRA Headquarters were at Seedaseer Lines, so named after the first battle honour of a battalion of the Mahratta Light Infantry, an Indian regiment which had been sent to reinforce Aden's garrison on the outbreak of the Second World War, which was quartered in Khormaksar. The APL had taken over the lines as a headquarters after the end of the war, which consequently became the headquarters of the FRA

During its short existence, the FRA continued the traditions of the APL and became a very professional military force. It continued to serve throughout the former Western Aden Protectorate, which was now known as the Federation of South Arabia. The Eastern Aden Protectorate never joined

Ferret Scout Cars of the FRA Armoured Car Squadron. Each vehicle is named after a South Arabian town. (Peter Herrett)

FRA artillery battery under training, 1966. (Peter Herrett)

FRA Ferret Scout Car preparing for a patrol. (Peter Herrett)

The FRA Armoured Car Squadron was equipped with Saladin Armoured Cars, which had a 76mm gun, before the British left Aden in 1967. (David Birtles)

FRA band (silver) and pipes March Past at Seedaseer Lines, 1967 (Tony Ford)

the Federation. Tactics and armament remained similar to that of the APL, although more emphasis was placed on motor transport and armoured cars. Saladin armoured cars were introduced about 1966–67 and a number of 25-pdr artillery pieces were supplied to the FRA during 1966 when training took place and were sent up-country to support the FRA the following year.

A major action with Arab dissidents in the Radfan Mountains was eventually contained due to increased assistance from British regiments because the FRA was overstretched. The main frontier garrisons were at Dhala, Mukheiras and Beihan. Arab nationalism was increasing throughout the area, and increased pressure from Egypt and the Yemen ensured that trouble was constantly brewing throughout the Federation. Following Britain's declaration to quit South Arabia, it appeared inevitable that the Federation would collapse and civil war would ensue. In an effort to unify the various armed forces in the country, it was decided to form the South Arabian Army (SAA), which would be based on an amalgamation of the Federal Regular Army and its old rival the Federal National Guard. It was planned that the Hadhrami Bedouin Legion would also come into this

FRA Bedford lorry fitted with an anti-aircraft cupola with a .50-inch M2 Browning heavy machine gun. (Tony Ford)

FRA fort and camp at Ataq in November 1965. (Peter Herrett)

grouping. On 1 June 1967, the FRA was redesignated as the South Arabian Army.

BAND

This band was a marching brass band capable of playing traditional British military music. A section of the band was trained in traditional Arab instruments and performed Arab music. The FRA band wore ceremonial dress.

UNIFORM

When up-country, the uniform of the FRA was similar to that of the APL, consisting of a khaki drill shirt and shorts, rolled down socks, brown plimsolls and a smart, small, Audhali khaki head cloth or *mashedda*. The white *pagri* of the APL was replaced by one of dark green for ceremonial purposes and a patch with a fringe worn on the left-hand side of the *pagri* in Federation colours. Ceremonial uniform comprised of a white button up tunic with dark green epaulets, white shorts, dark green cummerbund, dark green hosetops, khaki puttees with white ties, black boots. Unlike the APL, the FRA was issued with Arabic rank insignia, so that

FRA Signals Camel Section operating a C12 radio, 1965. (Royal Signals Museum)

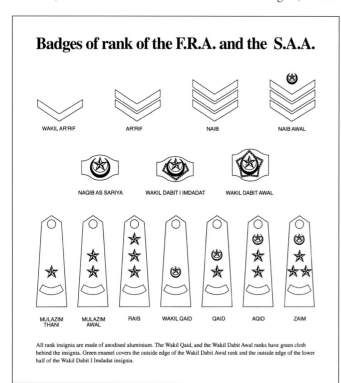

Badges of rank of the F.R.A. and the S.A.A.

WAKIL AR'RIF   AR'RIF   NAIB   NAIB AWAL

NAQIB AS SARIYA   WAKIL DABIT I IMDADAT   WAKIL DABIT AWAL

MULAZIM THANI   MULAZIM AWAL   RAIS   WAKIL QAID   QAID   AQID   ZAIM

All rank insignia are made of anodised aluminium. The Wakil Qaid, and the Wakil Dabit Awal ranks have green cloth behind the insignia. Green enamel covers the outside edge of the Wakil Dabit Awal rank and the outside edge of the lower half of the Wakil Dabit I Imdadat insignia.

(Malcolm Thomas)

Minister of Defence, Federation of South Arabia, 2nd February 1967, Front row L to R: Aqid Ahmed Muhammad Hassani, Commader Area East. Aqid Muhammad Ahmed Aulaqi MC, Deputy Commander FRA designate. H.H. Sulan Fadhl Bin Ali al Abdali, Minister of Defence. Zaim Jack B. Dye OBE, MC, Commander FRA. Aqid Nasser Buraik Aulaqi MBE Deputy Commander FRA. Back Row L to R: Col J.B. Chaplin DSO OBE retd Private Secretary to Minister of Defence. Qaid Salem Abdullah Abdalli, CO 4 FRA. Qaid Abdullah Ahmed Aulaqi MC, CO 2 FRA. Qaid Abdul Qawi Muhammad Maflahi, CO 1 FRA. Qaid Muhammad Said Yafai MBE, CO Training Bn FRA. Qaid Ali Abdullah Maisari, CO 5 FRA. (Tom Wylie)

FRA Ceremonial Camel Troop on parade at Seedaseer Lines with the FRA band between them. The Federation flag flies high. (Tony Ford)

March Past with Colours, FRA Seedaseer Lines, Aden. The officer with sword drawn is wearing the green and white lanyard from the Headquarters Battalion, which included the training battalion and band. (Tony Ford)

FRA WOII Said Omar astride a captured Yemeni BTR 40. (Peter Herret)

Inspection of the FRA Camel Troop, 1967. The flash and fringe on the headdress of the camel drivers is in the colours of the Federation flag. (Tony Ford)

WOII Peter Herrett FRA standing with a captured Yemeni BTR-40 Armoured Personnel Carrier at Dhala, 1966. (Peter Herrett)

Marchpast with colours, Seedaseer Lines, Aden. (Tony Ford)

Photo from a recruiting poster of a member of the FRA Ceremonial Camel Section. The lance carries a pennant which is dark green over white. The headdress is dark green as is the cummerbund, which is worn over a white tunic. A brown leather 1903 cavalry pattern bandoleer is strapped over the left shoulder. Dark green hosetops and khaki puttees are worn with black boots. (Bill Cranston)

Members of the FRA man a 106mm anti-tank gun while observed by officers and local dignitaries ca 1960s. (John Daymond)

the pips were replaced with stars, and the crown with stars and crescents. FRA forces had their own cap badge, which was similar to the old APL badge except that the crown was replaced by a star and crescent, and the scroll was in Arabic. An Arabic anodized aluminium shoulder title was worn along with anodized buttons, which featured the cap badge design. Officer's quality silver and gilt cap and collar badges were also produced and worn as well as an officer's wire wove headdress badge. A dark blue beret was issued. The khaki *pagri* with the old APL green and white flash with fringe continued to be worn with parade dress for some time after formation. A dark green stable belt was worn and dark green hosetops.

LANYARDS

HQ (including the Training Battalion and Band) – green and white twist
1st Battalion – orange
2nd Battalion – blue
3rd Battalion – red
4th Battalion – Cambridge blue
5th Battalion – White

The support squadrons wore the lanyard of the corresponding
Corps in the British Army

The 1st Battalion lanyard is recorded as gold, yellow and orange
in various documents, and 4th Battalion as Cambridge blue and
turquoise. All lanyards are three-ply rayon cord, 34 inches overall
with one-and-a-half-inch double loop at one end forming runner
and one inch (double) loop at the opposite end.

GOVERNMENT GUARDS

HARAS AL HAKOOMA

The Government Guards were a formation whose existence was
conceived by Major Basil W. Seager CMG, OBE, who was the first
Political Officer in 1937. He suggested to the government that a
frontier force of approximately 100 men should be formed. By
March 1938 approval had been received to raise the Government
Guards. It was intended that the force would also be used within
the Protectorate limits, in areas adjacent to the Yemen frontier
where there were likely to be inter-tribal disputes between tribes
living on either side of the border. It was decided that the force
should also be available for internal security work.

Captain R.A.B. Hamilton (later Lord Belhaven and Stenton)
became the first commander. Headquarters was constructed in
one of the numerous date gardens at Sheikh Othman, just outside
Aden. After a year it was planned to double the strength of the
Government Guards, and to include a troop of horse. The irregular
nature of the Government Guard is nicely put by Lord Belhaven
and Stenton in his book *The Uneven Road*. He described the men
as being older and more seasoned to the mischances of the world
than the men of the Levies – men of standing in their own tribe,
with their own characteristics which no parade discipline could
suppress. The Guards were unofficially known as 'Ham's Outfit'
or 'Ham's catch-em-aliveos'.

The Government Guards – a gendarmerie paid for by HM
Government – were deployed about the Western Aden Protectorate.
They were to be found along the frontier in a number of small
forts and provided escorts and static guards. On occasion, they
were able to provide support to various tribal guards. Because of
their wide deployment, and the police function which they had to
perform, they had less opportunity for formal training as soldiers.
Consequently, the Guards were less technically competent than
the Aden Protectorate Levies, although their respective purpose
and organisation were quite different. More lightly armed than
the Levies, the Guards possessed Jordan-trained Arab officers who
were promoted to appointments formerly held by British officers.
The 'Arabisation' of the Guards created a different military
environment to that of the Levies, who were based on British
regular infantry lines. This became a problem in later years as the
Levies regarded themselves as the more professional force. In 1938,
Government Guards were given the additional task of guarding
vital points, with prime responsibility for the Aden pipeline and
water supply. Patrol duties included a car patrol, which consisted
of one *rais* (captain) and six *askaris* (soldiers). Every two hours two
men were to patrol in the car from Government Guards Garden
(headquarters) at Sheikh Othman to the Isthmus parapets. A camel
patrol, consisting of a *rais* and six *askaris*, patrolled every two hours
from the Levy fence via Government Guards' Headquarters to Bir
Fadhl. A post of three men was stationed at Khormaksar Bridge,
where the water pipe emerged to the surface of the ground. A

further six posts were located at the wells of the Government
Guards' Garden. Each post consisted of three men.

From 1940 until the Italian surrender in East Africa 'Ham's
Outfit' also contained a naval element. This consisted of the crews
of four small *dhows* fitted with auxiliary engines. These were used
to harry the small Italian-occupied ports on the Somali coast and
to blockade the Straits of Bab al Mandeb. They mounted two-
pounder guns and with a lucky shot one succeeded in sinking a
German cargo ship trying to escape from the Red Sea by night.
The naval commander in Aden refused to acknowledge these
vessels as coming under his command, describing them as a
bunch of pirates, and would not allow them to fly the naval
ensign. Consequently, the flotilla commander, an Irishman, flew
the Cross of St. Patrick.

By the early 1950s the strength of the Guards had reached over
500 men, who were dispersed in numerous posts throughout
the Western Aden Protectorate. Headquarters moved to a
small reserve at Khormaksar in Aden Colony, and the unit was
commanded by a British Commandant, four British and 14 Arab
officers. Depending on the terrain, the soldiers travelled either
on foot, camel or lorry. Recruitment was from all tribes in the
Western Aden Protectorate, no segregation occurred. Many of the
permanent posts were in some of the most inaccessible parts of
the Protectorate, but contact was maintained by means of wireless
telegraphy. In 1959, with the creation of the Amirates of the
South, the Government Guards and Tribal Guard merged. The
new force was titled the Federal National Guard. Weapons used
by the Government Guards were the .303 Rifle SMLE No. 1 Mk
III, Bren Gun and a few 3-inch mortars.

UNIFORM

The original uniform of the Government Guards was the war
dress of the Mushreq tribes (eastern tribes from Awaliq and
Wahidi). This consisted of a loin cloth, head cloth and plaid of
indigo blue, with a dagger and a cartridge belt. A blue bush shirt
was also worn. For desert work all of this was covered with a khaki
head cloth and smock. Boots were not worn. Later, the Guards
wore distinctive uniforms consisting of khaki shorts and shirt, a
leather belt superimposed on a khaki cummerbund, puttees and
sandals of local manufacture. Headdress consisted of a black *pagri*
with a green flash on the left-hand side, superimposed on which
was the crossed rifles cap badge. By the late 1950s, parade dress
was modified to include black boots, black leather equipment
and ammunition carriers, which carried loose ammunition rather
than clips. A black belt was worn over a dark green cummerbund.
The black *pagri* was retained and included the green flash on the
left-hand side with a blackened Government Guards cap badge.
In the field, a khaki *mashedda* or a large khaki beret (soup-plate
style) was worn. Officers'-quality cap badges were of blackened
brass or bronze, while other ranks cap badges were of cast brass
and came without a crown. The headdress badge was approved
on 23 January 1946 and issued in 1947. Worn at first in black it
was worn by all Arab ranks on a green flash on the left side of
the *pagri* and by British officers on the left side of the bush hat.
Buttons were black and bore the king's crown and GG on them.
The back was stamped 'FIRMIN LONDON'. A skill-at-arms
badge, 'Marksman', consisted of crossed rifles, embroidered in
black mercerised cotton on khaki drill. This was sealed by Crown
Agents on 24 September 1957. A khaki cloth shoulder title, with
GOVERNMENT GUARDS written in black Arabic script was
worn at the top of the sleeve, which was approved 7 September

1954. This replaced the copper-bronze GG shoulder titles which wore very badly and were damaged by the rifle sling causing the blacking to wear off. See illustration in badge section.

GOOD CONDUCT PAY AND BADGES 1 APRIL 1947

Reward for good conduct and efficient and faithful service. The badge was an inverted chevron with the maximum permitted being three, worn on the lower half of the left sleeve. These badges were awarded for two years of good service. This badge

was not worn by NCOs. The Commandant could award badges for special service.

GOVERNMENT GUARD FLAG

All Government Guards Posts in the Protectorate flew a flag which was green with the badge in black in the centre. Approved 23 January 1946.

Government Guard Fort at As Sarir WAP during the mid-1950s. (Tom Wylie)

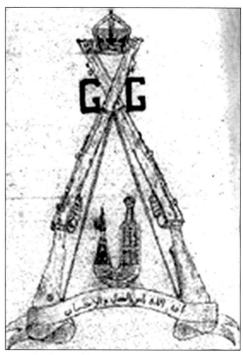

Original drawing for the headdress badge of the Government Guards in bronze dated 1946. (British Library)

Table 7: Titles and badges of rank for the Government Guard

Title	Rank	Insignia
Approved 4 March 1940:		
Amir	Senior Government Guards officer	
Rais Mia	Junior Government Guards officer	
After 1 April 1940 the Tribal Guard Instructors became Government Guards officers. New ranks were approved:		
Qaid	Senior Arab officer	Crown
Rais	Salary Rs.100/- or over	3 Stars
Mulazim Awal	Salary of Rs.80/- or over But below Rs.100/-	2 Stars
Mulazim Thani	Salary below Rs.80/-	1 Star
Sergeant Major	Naqib	Crown on sleeve
Sergeant	Naib	3 Chevrons
Corporal	Areef	2 Chevrons
Lance Corporal	Wakil Areef	1 Chevron
Guard	Jundi	
Officer Rank badges worn in 1955:		
Commandant		Crown and Star
Deputy Commandant & Qaid Assistant Commandant	(Over 900 Pounds per annum)	Crown
Assistant Commandants	(Under 900 Pounds per annum)	3 Stars
Mulazim Awal		2 Stars
Mulazim Thani		1 Star
(Approval for all Assistant Commandants to wear three stars on the epaulets granted on 14 December 1955)		

Government Guard fort at Merta, WAP, May 1958. The fort was located about 2,000 yards from the Yemeni military border town of Am Soumah. The Land Rover and crew are APL. This fort featured in a number of border incidents. (Major C. Butt)

Government Guards at Merta Fort WAP, June 1958. Two are in full uniform, i.e. black leather equipment, dark green cummerbund, black *mashedda* with green flash and fringe and GG cap badge. They are armed with SMLE No1 Mk III rifles. Note the ammunition carriers in place of British army pouches. Two other soldiers are in working dress and wear khaki berets with a GG badge on a green flash. Their locally made ammunition belts are for carrying separate cartridges rather than clips. (Major C. Butt)

HADHRAMI BEDOUIN LEGION

AL JAISH AL BADAWI AL HADRAMI

Modelled on the successful Arab Legion, the Hadhrami Bedouin Legion (HBL) was formed in 1940 as a British military force to be used in the Eastern Aden Protectorate. The HBL was an all-Arab regiment, paid for by Britain and used as the Resident Adviser's own force until 1956, after which a British officer commanded the force. Bedouin tribesmen were recruited to form a light infantry that was tough and highly mobile in difficult terrain.

In 1936 Harold Ingrams was appointed Resident Adviser to the Hadhramaut States and British Agent, Eastern Aden Protectorate. His main concern was to end the endemic tribal warfare. By using the successful establishment of the Arab Legion as his model, Ingrams was able to produce a similar force. In 1939, three Jordanian officers on secondment from the Arab Legion arrived in the Hadhramaut, and the first 50 tribesmen were recruited and trained at the HBL Liejun post at Gheil bin Yumain in Hamumi tribal territory. The fort was built in similar fashion to the desert posts of Glubb Pasha's Arab Legion in Trans-Jordan. A wireless station was installed to provide communications with Mukalla, but the remoteness was a disadvantage, headquarters consequently moved to Dis, near Mukalla. Leijun was the Headquarters of the HBL but later became an outpost, and as men became available, further outposts were manned at Bir Asakir and Al Abr. Many of the forts had a 'Beau Geste' appearance. In 1940, the HBL comprised 42 all ranks at the Headquarters, augmented with a detachment of Katheri Armed Constabulary. Transport included two trucks and 12 camels. Rais Barakat was the first commandant, and his second-in-command was Khalid.

In about 1947 these two officers were recalled to Jordan and Abdul Hadi Hammad took command. Later, a more senior Arab Legion officer, Qaid Naif al Faiz, was brought in to take command. During the famine years of 1944 and 1948, the HBL was used for the distribution of famine relief supplies. After the famine there was a fresh outbreak of 'dissidence' in the remoter western areas of the Plateau and in Wadis Amd and Irma. These were successfully quelled by a combined force of MRA and HBL under the command of the MARA Major I.E. (Jock) Snell. Rais Abdul Hadi (Jordanian) also distinguished himself by running operations using troops of both forces without discrimination. Qaid Naif al Faiz was involved in the expansion of the HBL and this very able officer was tasked with eliminating cross-border raiding and feuding in the Northern Deserts, which had been going on since time immemorial.

In 1950 three more forts were built at Zamakh, Minwakh, and Markaz Hajr and patrols from them kept the Seiar and Kurab under control. However, the patrols were inadequate for the eastern tribes, collectively known as Al Mishqas. They had grievances with the Dahm and Abida of North Yemen, and the Yam from Saudi Arabia who had treated them brutally in the past. In November 1951, a combined raiding force of Minhali and Mahri tribesmen watered at Thamud some 150 miles east of Minwakh. There had been good rains and there were temporary waterholes north and east of the HBL forts. Using the waterholes and carrying enough water for human consumption they followed the sands of the Empty Quarter in an arc round the string of outcrops known as Raiyan, the eastern extremity of the territory of the Dahm where they captured a waterhole known as Mashainiqa. From Mashainiqa they raided not only the Dahm, but the Abida and Yam tribes, and then dashed off back home along the same route that they had come. Abdul Hadi had intelligence of the raiding party and commandeered some vehicles at gunpoint from the Desert Locust Control and set off in pursuit. The HBL caught up with some of the raiders at Shaqham killing two and recaptured some of the stolen loot.

The strength of the HBL was now about 170 and doubled over the next two of years. HBL schools were built for both boys and girls,

HBL outside the guardhouse at the British Residency. HBL in the front wear the white ceremonial attire while those in the background are in khaki. Col Hugh Bousted (British Agent and Resident Adviser) is dressed in British Colonial Office uniform ca 1954. (Sultan Ghalib)

HBL Ferret Scout Cars in the Hadhramaut ca 1960. (Mrs Snell)

before either moving on to another area, or into reserve at Headquarters. By this time the HBL outnumbered both the Mukalla Regular Army (MRA) and Qu'aiti Armed Constabulary (QAC) combined. Qu'aiti forces were left to maintain peace and order in the settled areas of the State, including the north-west plateau while the HBL were used to back-up the States and the huge area of desert and mountain beyond. Heavier weapons were introduced, and four Ferret Scout Cars were acquired in 1960. At the time that the Federation was being formed the eastern States had already combined their forces against mutual danger, and saw little advantage in joining what they looked upon as a gaggle of small districts whose administrations had a long way to go before they reached the condition of those of the Qu'aiti and Kathiri.

The eastern Sultanate of Mahra was technically a part of the Eastern Aden Protectorate, and had its Sultan on Socotra Island, many miles from the State proper. In reality, Mahra was an enormous area which had seen very few Europeans. Although a treaty had been signed with the Sultan, he did not speak for all of the people, and the State was a lawless area into which few outsiders dared to venture. Oil exploration was the incentive required to establish a British presence in the area. In the early 1960s, a force of the HBL managed to establish a company-strength fort at Al Gheidha, the capital of Mahra. Another fort was built at Marait, and a small State force (Tribal Guard) was also raised. Major David Eales, second-in-command, was murdered at Marait by a Hamumi *jundi* who held a grudge against him – the murderer escaped. The following year Pat Gray, the Commandant, was ambushed and died of his wounds. Colonel Eric Johnson, Military Adviser to the Resident Adviser, took over command with Wakil Qaid Salim Umar al Johi as second-in-command. The force remained loyal to its paymasters, and in 1967 mounted a successful operation utilising RAF Beverley aircraft to flush out all National Liberation Front (NLF) supporters on Socotra Island. With great flair the HBL captured the entire Mahra NLF hierarchy. After the British left Aden, the HBL and other local forces were, with varying degrees

and famine orphans were given the chance to gain an education. Many of the students went on to become wireless operators, clerks and mechanics in the force. Thamud Well was occupied in 1953, Sanau in 1954, and Habarut, on the Omani border, in 1956. That year a considerable number of HBL were employed as escorts to the oil exploration parties. At this time it was decided that it was essential to pacify the notoriously combative Mahra to make administration possible there, a thing previously unheard of. Naif returned to Jordan in 1955, and was replaced by Khalaf Qaftan, but he too was recalled in 1957. Jock Snell of the Royal Sussex Regiment became commandant for a short period, after which a South African, Pat Gray, took command. He reorganised the HBL into what amounted to infantry companies, with each company being assigned an area of responsibility for six months

Aden Police piper as of 1966: the Band and Ceremonial Guard wore a white tunic and shorts with red *pagri* and *shamla*, black *khulla*, black hosetops with red turnovers, and black boots. British-style bandsman badges and piper's badges were worn on the sleeves. (Artwork by David Birtles)

Aden Protectorate Levies Ceremonial Guard *shawoosh* in 1956. The red stripe at the front of the white *pagri*, made this soldier recognisable as a member of the Ceremonial Guard, trained to very high British Army standards. The green flash was worn with a white horizontal bar on APL *pagri*, which was both khaki and white. (Artwork by David Birtles)

The Aden Armed Police was a smart, disciplined, and well-trained battalion-sized force deployed for riot control and guard duties within Aden. This was one of its Armed Policemen as of 1965. (Artwork by David Birtles)

The Federal Regular Army (FRA) possessed a large marching band, with a smart turn out and capable of playing quality music. The band uniform was the same as the Ceremonial Guard, including a white tunic and shorts, and a green *pagri* with the flash in the colours of the Federation. This was one of its Drum Majors. (Artwork by David Birtles)

Mulazim Awal of the Federal National Guard (FNG), as of 1960. He is shown wearing the black FNG *sedara* or forage hat, with a green crown and green piping. The officer's white metal headdress badge was placed at the front of the hat. Leather equipment was all locally-manufactured. (Artwork by David Birtles)

A soldier of the FRA Ceremonial Camel Troop, as of 1965. Formerly the Aden Protectorate Levies Camel Troop, and with a proud history almost going back to the times of the Aden Troop, this unit was used for ceremonial duties only, including escort and military parade. (Artwork by David Birtles)

An *Arrif* of the Federal National Guard, as of 1960. The FNG was akin to a gendarmerie, rather than a regiment of the regular army. Most of its officers and other ranks were Arab, and they served exclusively within the Aden Protectorate, providing guards for numerous forts within the different states and conducting convoy escorts and border patrols. (Artwork by David Birtles)

The Government Guard was the forerunner of the FNG and paid for by Her Majesty's Government. Its troops had tasks similar to those of an armed rural police, were lightly armed and deployed only within the Aden Protectorate. (Artwork by David Birtles)

This *Mulazim Awal* of the Hadhrami Bedouin Legion (HBL) is shown in a ceremonial white uniform (Crown Agents issue) worn as of 1967. Originally raised along the lines of the Arab Legion in Transjordan, the HBL were paid by the British, and had a function similar to that of a light infantry regiment: lightly armed but highly mobile, they were deployed within the Eastern Protectorate and closely cooperated with the EAP. (Artwork by David Birtles)

The Kahtiri State in the Eastern Aden Protectorate was less powerful than the Qu'aiti State, but had its own armed force – the Kathiri Armed Constabulary, a *jundi* of which is shown as they would have appeared in 1966. Units from the Eastern Aden Protectorate proved more professional than those from the west, and worked hand-in-hand with each other. (Artwork by David Birtles)

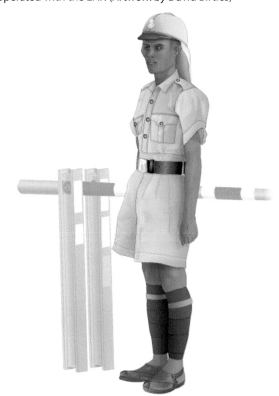

An officer of the Lahej Police, 1959. Like most police officers in Southern Arabia, he wore the ubiquitous khaki tunic and shorts, but was readily recognised by very distinctive headdress, similar to the helmet of the Jordanian Police, but without a spike on top. A brass headdress badge was worn at the front of the helmet. (Artwork by David Birtles)

A *rais* of the Lahej Trained Force (LTF), 1955: the service probably reached its zenith in the mid-1940s, when it was a smart outfit with a good degree of training. While its uniform was classic in appearance (the LTF mirrored the Mukalla Regular Army), it was distinguishable by the red *pagri* flash, and fringe with a white bar. No metal badges or shoulder titles were worn. (Artwork by David Birtles)

A *jundi* of the Mukalla Regular Army (MRA), 1955. Standing at ease, he is shown wearing the ceremonial dress, notable for the red *pagri*, red lanyard, and red *usra* under the leather belt. Red was a link to the earlier uniforms and the Arab Regiment of Hyderabad. Well disciplined, the MRA was trained as light infantry. (Artwork by David Birtles)

The Mukalla Regular Army (MRA) was the regiment of H. H. Sultan Ghalib of Qu'aiti. Based in Mukalla, it was a well-trained and disciplined force, familiar with most of the Eastern Aden Protectorate. This shows a *wakil quaid* of the MRA in 1966. (Artwork by David Birtles)

The MRA had its own Camel Troop, which served for ceremonial and guard purposes, and this illustration shows the uniform and insignia of an MRA camel lancer of the Qu'aiti Sultan's Ceremonial Guard. (Artwork by David Birtles)

This was the ceremonial uniform of a MRA lieutenant in 1935. (Artwork by David Birtles)

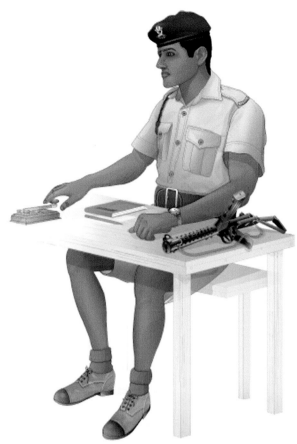

This illustration shows H. H. Sultan Ghalib in the summer uniform of the *Musheer* (Commander-in-Chief) of the Qu'aiti Armed Forces, as of 1966. The uniform includes a white tunic and black cavalry trousers with a gold stripe, with boots and spurs. The Order of the Hadhramaut is visible along with the Qu'aiti DSM and MSM. The headress was that of an officer of the Mukalla Regular Army, without cap badge. (Artwork by David Birtles)

The South Arabian Army (SAA) had an extensive voice and Morse network across the Federation, with the main communications centre located at Seedaseer Lines in Aden. A small Royal Signals teleprinter detachment provide a point-to-point link into 15 Signal Regiment at Singapore Lines in Aden. This SAA signaller is shown as he would have appeared in 1967: notable is the dark blue lanyard of the SAA Signal Squadron around his right shoulder. (Artwork by David Birtles)

A *naib* of the Qu'aiti Armed Constabulary as of 1965. Paid for by the Qu'aiti State, this was a reliable, well-trained rural armed police force, which generally proved better than all others outside of Aden. (Artwork by David Birtles)

The platoon-sized Qu'aiti Sultanic Guard was charged with protecting the Sultan and wore a uniform designed by Sultan Ghalib II. They were provided with British Army self-loading rifles (SLRs) and were well-trained in their use. (Artwork by David Birtles)

This soldier from 3 Para is shown armed with a 9mm Sterling submachine gun and carrying a 3.5-inch rocket launcher during operations in Radfan of April and June 1964. (Artwork by Renato Dalmaso)

A soldier of 1st Battalion East Anglian Regiment as seen while escorting supplies in Radfan in 1964. He is armed with the 7.62mm L1A1 SLR; a semi-automatic British variant of the FN FAL. (Artwork by Renato Dalmaso)

An airman of the RAF as seen during a parade at RAF Khormaksar in 1943. (Artwork by Renato Dalmaso)

A machine gun team of the Coldstream Guards seen firing a 7.62mm GPMG during the fighting in the mountains of the Western Aden Protectorate in January 1965. (Artwork by Renato Dalmaso)

4001 Flight of the RAF, deployed for the protection of RAF Aden, was equipped with Otter armoured cars, manufactured in Canada during the Second World War. They were lightly armoured and had an armament consisting of a hull-mounted Boys anti-tank rifle, and a Bren machine gun. Except for registration plates – applied in white on a black background, painted directly on the front of the lower hull – they wore only a simple insignia in white and an RAF roundal on the front and back, leaving no doubts about their owners. Other vehicles of this unit wore the same insignia applied on the doors of the drivers' cabs. (Artwork by David Bocquelet)

No fewer than 4,409 Ferret scout cars were manufactured in Great Britain between 1952 and 1962, and they saw widespread service in the Aden Protectorate. The Hadhrami Bedouin Legion (HBL) was equipped with a squadron of Ferrets: left in green overall, these were unusual in so far that their turret (mounting a machine gun) was elevated through insertion of an armoured superstructure. (Artwork by David Bocquelet)

In addition to the HBL, the APL and the FRA also operated a number of Ferret armoured cars. Most were left in overall green and only a few painted in yellow sand overall. As shown in the insets, APL vehicles wore registration plates in black with white Arabic digits and numerals above the front driver's hatch, and had white inscriptions on the turret. Tactical insignia (a square in red and yellow) was usually applied low on the hull. (Artwork by David Bocquelet)

Bedford RL lorries were the main medium trucks of the British Army and allied forces in the Aden Protectorate during the 1960s. Some examples operated by the FRA had a cupola with a Browning M2 heavy machine gun atop the driver's cab. Generally left in green overall, they received the tactical insignia of that service – a square in green and white – on the right front bumper. Bedfords operated by the HBL (shown on the right) were painted in black overall, had a thick red stripe over the engine compartment, and that unit's crest on both doors of the driver's cab. (Artwork by David Bocquelet)

Like its Bedford lorries, Land Rovers of the HBL were painted in black overall and had a wide stripe in red across their engine compartment for easier identification from the air. Many also received the crest of the HBL on the doors of the driver's compartment. The service title was worn in white, on a red square, on the left front bumper. FRA Land Rovers had a similar appearance but wore the tactical insignia in green and white on the front of the right bumper, and registrations (for example: 27BS07, 46BP22, or 05DL12) on the left bumper. (Artwork by David Bocquelet)

This BTR-40 armoured car was one of 100 acquired by the Imamate of Yemen from the USSR in 1956 or 1957. It was captured by British forces during one of many border skirmishes of the 1962-1967 period and pressed into service with the APL. While still in its overall green livery, it received the service crest and a yellow square at the upper front armoured plate, indicating it belonged to 1 Battalion FRA. (Artwork by David Bocquelet)

After the end of the Second World War, the RAF deployed Tempest F.Mk VIs from No. 8 Squadron – some of the most powerful piston-engined fighter-bombers of that conflict – to Aden. The first batch of aircraft (for example NX154 and NX237) still wore the standardised camouflage pattern in dark sea grey (BS381C/638) and dark green (BS381C/641) on top surfaces. Later on, all were repainted in high-speed silver overall, with spinners in black, as shown here. Typical armament consisted of internal cannons and up to eight unguided 127mm rockets. Bombs were carried rarely, but examples up to 1,000lbs were observed in service. Tempests of No. 8 Squadron flew air strikes in support of ground forces until 1949, when the unit converted to de Haviland Brigands. (Artwork by Tom Cooper)

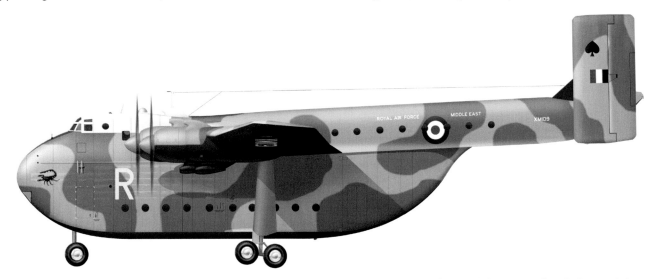

Developed in the early 1950s, the Blackburn Beverley C.Mk 1 heavy transport was the result of a search for an aircraft with the capability to carry oversized loads, and retain short-take-off and landing capabilities. It had a huge cargo area with large doors at the rear, above which was a deck where it could carry 94 troops or 75 paratroopers. Only 47 were manufactured, but they served with five squadrons. One of these – No. 84 – flew Beverleys from RAF Khormaksar from 1958 until 1967. All of that unit's aircraft wore a standardised camouflage pattern in light stone (BS381C/361) and dark earth (BS381C/350) on upper surfaces and sides, and black on undersides. Code was applied in medium grey on the forward fuselage, with – in addition to the unit's insignia (a black scorpion) on the nose – individual aircraft having playing card symbols on the fin: for example a diamond on XM103/V, a club on XM107/P and a spade in this case (XM109/R). (Artwork by Tom Cooper)

The Westland (Bristol) Belvedere HC.Mk 1 was developed in the early 1950s, and was powered by two engines connected by a shaft so that, in the event that one failed, both rotors continued turning. The Belvedere had a large sliding door on the right side of the fuselage and was capable of lifting either 18 troops or 2,722kg internal cargo, or underslung cargo of up to 2,381kg. The RAF acquired only 24 helicopters of this type, but they saw intensive operational service – including in Aden, where No. 26 Squadron operated them from 1963 until 1965. All were painted in Transport Command's colour scheme, including white on upper surfaces, and aluminium-silver elsewhere. (Artwork by Tom Cooper)

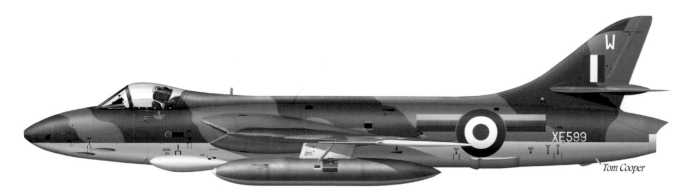

As well as the Hunter FGA.Mk 9, the RAF also operated Hunter FR.Mk 10s in the Aden Protectorate. The principal task of this version was photo-reconnaissance, for which it had a revised nose section containing five cameras. Like FGA.Mk 9s, FR.Mk 10s wore the standardised camouflage pattern in dark green and dark sea grey over, and silver on undersurfaces. Serials were applied in black or white on the rear fuselage, and codes in white near the top of the fin, while squadron markings surrounded the roundel on the rear fuselage. No. 43 Squadron, RAF, operated Hawker Hunter FGA.Mk 9 fighter-bombers from Khormaksar between 1963 and 1967. (Artwork by Tom Cooper)

Westland Wessex helicopters became the principal medium transport and assault platforms of both the RAF and the Fleet Air Arm during the mid-1960s. The latter regularly forward deployed detachments from various units to Aden, starting in 1964. This Wessex HU.Mk 5 from NAS 845 Fleet Air Arm was one of the helicopters of this type to cover the evacuation from the Aden Protectorate in 1967, by when it could be armed with machine guns and launchers for unguided rockets. While RAF-operated examples were usually painted in dark grey and dark green, and the FAA's in yellow over and blue-grey under, this example (serial XS523) received a camouflage pattern in light stone and olive drab (BS381C/298), and a large NAS 845 crest behind the cockpit. (Artwork by Tom Cooper

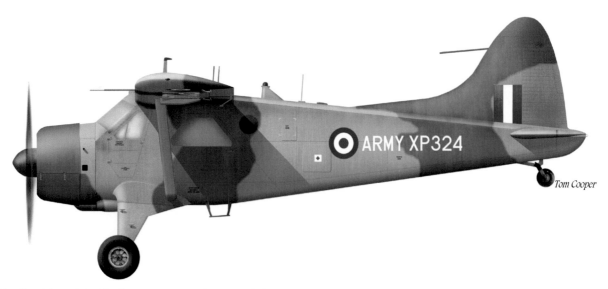

The de Havilland Canada DHC-2 Beaver was a single-engined short-take-off and landing aircraft developed for operations under most primitive conditions. The Army Air Corps acquired 46 aircraft designated Beaver AL.Mk 1, and deployed them as utility transports: No. 15 Flight operated them over much of the Western Aden Protectorate, successfully coping with even the most primitive landing strips. All of the AAC's Beavers were painted in dark earth (BS381C/350) overall, with a standardised camouflage pattern in dark green (BS381C/641) on top surfaces and sides. Other markings were rather simple, and included the national insignia and serials, but some examples received white bands on the mid-wing, for easier identification. (Artwork by Tom Cooper)

Ataq Airstrip, with FNG officers and men in the foreground, ca 1961. Note the sergeant wearing green overalls and a cotton bandoleer around his waist. (Jim Ellis)

Aden Protectorate Levies Ceremonial Guard Camel Troop. (Major C.A. Stahelin)

Aden Protectorate Levies Camel Troop in Aden, ca 1959. (Major C.A. Stahelin)

Aden Protectorate Ferret armoured car, ca 1959. Note the badge painted on its side. (David Birtles)

Aden Protectorate Levies marching with bayonets fixed on Rifles No.4 Mk. 1, ca 1959. The red stripe on the white headdress denotes membership of the Ceremonial Guard. (Major C.A. Stahelin)

Federal Regular Army Ceremonial Camel Troop, 1966 (Tony Ford)

Lancers of the Ceremonial Camel Troop of the Federal Regular Army. (Tony Ford)

Camel Troop South Arabian Army, Seedaseer Lines, 1967 (Tony Ford)

Federal Regular Army Camel Troop on parade at Seedaseer Lines Aden. (Tony Ford)

Federal Regular Army Band at Seedaseer Lines Aden ca 1966. (Tom Ford)

Federal Regular Army Camel Troop. (Major A.H. Fraser)

Federal Regular Army mortar section. The mortar is a British Ordnance 3-inch with Mk V barrel, No. 6 baseplate, Mk V bipod and utilises the Mk II sight. The bombs are probably HE rounds, identifiable by the flat round 162 fuse. Rifles No.4 Mk I are being carried. (Major C.A. Stahelin)

Fort at Dhala, early 1960s. (Jim Ellis)

Clerk of G Branch South Arabian Army. Note the SAA cap badge and shoulder title and the HQ lanyard. Seedaseer Lines, 1967. (Tony Ford)

Federal National Guard in 1963. Note the darkened '37 pattern webbing and khaki putties with black hosetops. (Jonathan Pittaway)

Federal National Guard officers, Sharif Haider in centre, ca 1961. Note the *sedara* hat with FNG hat badge in the front. (Jim Ellis)

Sultan Saleh bin Hussain al Audhali, Federal Minister of Security, visiting a FNG outpost during the early 1960s. Behind him flies the flag of the Federation. (Jim Ellis)

Officers outside the British Residency Mukalla, early 1960s. Left to right; Rais Saleh bin Salaan, Katheri Armed Constabulary; Rais Yusaf al Kathiri, Hadhrami Bedouin Legion; Rais Shaikh Azzani, Hadhrami Bedouin Legion, Signals; Sheikh Amin Kathiri State Secretary. (Jim Ellis)

Two Mukalla Regular Army officers, ca 1960. A Qu'aiti State award is worn by Captain Rubaiya, ADC to the Sultan (centre). All ranks wore British rank insignia. The MRA wore khaki Indian-style turbans with *khulla* and *shamla*. (Edith Grey)

The Mukalla Regular Army, distinguished by their red turbans, giving 'eyes right' whilst on parade at the British Residency in Mukalla, ca 1960. A Mukalla Sultanate bandsman can be seen to the right of the picture. (Jim Ellis)

Senior military and police officers prepare to review a parade in the compound of the British Residency in Mukalla, ca 1964. Left to right: O.C. Military Academy wearing a khaki/yellow beret and red epaulets; O.C. Civil Police; C.O. Qu'aiti Armed Constabulary; C.O. Mukalla Regular Army; Commander Qu'aiti Forces. (Saleh bin Someida. (Jim Ellis)

Hadhrami Bedouin Legion soldiers smartly turned out, ca 1960. Note the black leather belt with brass buckle with HBL insignia stamped on it. They have a yellow over red underlay beneath the shoulder title. (Edith Grey)

Hadhrami Bedouin Legion officers take a break, ca 1960. The intricate locally-made soft leather equipment can be seen clearly. Red HBL lanyards are worn. This rifle company has a black cloth underlay beneath the shoulder title. (Edith Grey)

Hadhrami Bedouin Legion barracks, situated on the outskirts of Mukalla, ca 1960. The city was the capital of Qu'aiti State in the Hadhramaut and the largest in the Eastern Aden Protectorate. The soldiers stand beside the HBL monument, bearing the Legion's badge painted onto it with the backing red over white. Flanking either side of it are Austrian Schwarzlose machine guns, which were acquired following the Italian surrender in Eritrea during the Second World War. They had originally belonged to the Austro-Hungarian army during the First World War, and had found their way into Italian service. Ammunition and belts had run out by 1952 and the weapons were replaced by .303 Bren guns. Behind the monument stands the Legion's flagpole. The buildings in the background are the Legion's administrative offices. (Edith Grey)

Federal Regular Army parading each battalions' standard. Mid-1960s. (Tony Ford)

Qu'aiti Armed Constabulary being inspected at the British Residency, Mukalla c.1964. They are wearing khaki uniform with a khaki imama and black aqu'al. HBL and MRA troops parade on their right. (Jim Ellis)

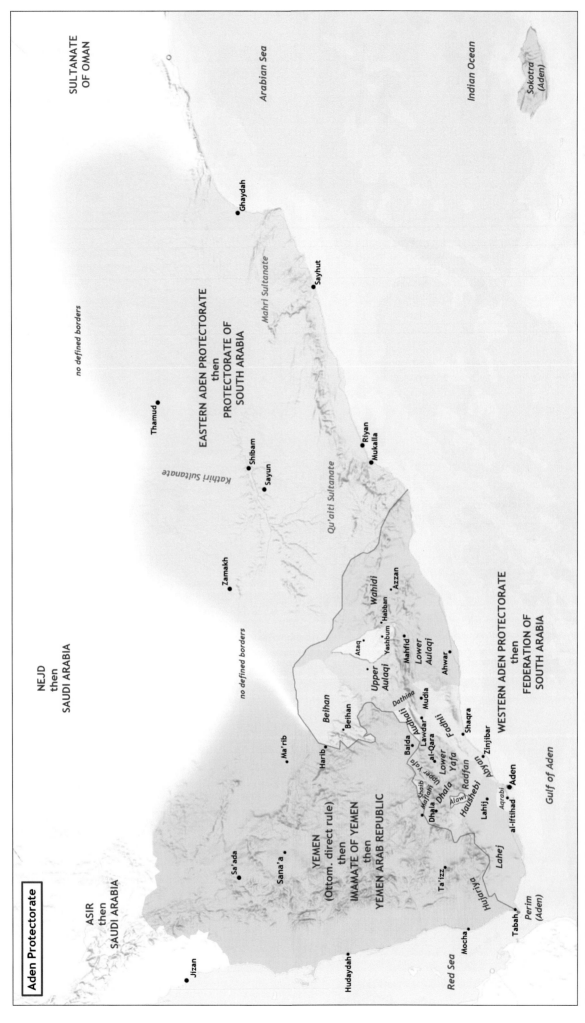

Aden Protectorate

NEJD
then
SAUDI ARABIA

ASIR
then
SAUDI ARABIA

SULTANATE
OF OMAN

Arabian Sea

no defined borders

Mahri Sultanate

EASTERN ADEN PROTECTORATE
then
PROTECTORATE OF
SOUTH ARABIA

Ghaydah

Sayhut

Thamud

Kathiri Sultanate

Shibam

Sayun

Qu'aiti Sultanate

Riyan

Mukalla

Zamakh

no defined borders

Wahidi

Azzan

Habban

Ataq

Yashbum

Mahfid

Upper
Aulaqi

Lower
Aulaqi

Ahwar

Dathina

WESTERN ADEN PROTECTORATE
then
FEDERATION OF
SOUTH ARABIA

Beihan

Beihan

Audhali

Lawdar

Mudia

Baida

al-Qara

Fadhli

Shaqra

Zinjibar

Ma'rib

Harib

Lower
Yafa

Upper Yafa

Jaddh

Radfan

Alawi

Abyan

Shaib

Maflahi

Dhala

Dhala

Hau shebi

Lahij

Aqrabi

al-Ifthad

Aden

Gulf of Aden

YEMEN
(Ottom. direct rule)
then
IMAMATE OF YEMEN
then
YEMEN ARAB REPUBLIC

Sa'ada

Sana'a

Ta'izz

Lahej

Hujariya

Perim
(Aden)

Tabah

Mocha

Hudaydah

Jizan

Red Sea

Indian Ocean

Sokotra
(Aden)

A map of the Aden Protectorate in the 1940s–1960s. Notably, the Western Aden Protectorate lasted until 1959, when five states united into the Federation of the Emirates of the South. Additional states – emirates and republics – joined later, while some never did. When Aden – a Crown Colony until 1963 (and including the immediate area, such as Little Aden, Sheikh Othman and al-Mansoura) – joined the Federation of Emirates of the South, the Federation of South Arabia was created. The area further east was called the Eastern Aden Protectorate for about a month or so before the end of the British presence, in 1967. (Map by Tom Cooper)

of success, absorbed into the People's Democratic Republic of Yemen armed forces.

UNIFORM

A light brown, calf-length *qamees* (*kamis*), or outer shirt, of khaki drill (Crown Agents SD2) was the original HBL uniform, while parade dress was white. In about 1958 the *qamees* was superseded by a khaki shirt and shorts, however the white *qamees* was retained as dress for parades. Soldiers wore a red canvas cummerbund, which had a sash on the left-hand side. Over the cummerbund was worn a HBL leather ammunition belt, which had a flat brass buckle bearing the HBL inscription. Headdress consisted of a red check *imama* (*kufiya*), which was similar to the headdress of the Arab Legion. The *imama* was held in place by a black goat's hair *aqu'al*; this is a camel hobble, which is tied in between a camel's forefeet with two strings, these hanging down the back when the *aqu'al* is worn on a man's head. Footwear was not issued until 1954, when a contingent was sent to Aden for the Queen's Visit. Sandals, of the type issued to the Government Guards, were issued to the contingent to protect their feet from Aden's tarred roads. Footwear was again issued in 1960, when the HBL and MRA were involved in suppression of a tribal war. In the field, officers usually wore much the same uniform as the men, but when in Mukalla, long trousers, tunic and brown shoes were often worn and on suitable occasions, a highly polished Sam Browne. Revolvers were not generally used, as the rifle was considered the mark of a man.

The design of the brass headdress badge, worn on the *aqu'al*, was a wreath with two crossed *jambias*, points uppermost, and a scroll with the inscription JAISH AL BADIYAH AL HADHRAMIYAH (Hadhrami Bedouin Legion) in Arabic script. This badge was later superseded by a locally made white metal badge, bearing the inscription JAISH AL BADIYAH (Bedouin Legion) in Arabic script. Brass (and later white metal) shoulder titles were designed by Qu'aiti Sultan Saleh bin Ghalib, whose hobbies included calligraphy. A red piece of cloth was worn under the shoulder title. When Colonel Gray reorganised the Legion he introduced single colour underlays for each rifle company, blue and white for signals, and red and blue for transport. Photographic evidence shows that the rifle company colours included red, black, gold/yellow, blue and green. Officers wore a red lanyard on the left shoulder.

SCHOOLS

There were both a Boys and a Girls school for HBL soldiers as well as a State Bedouin Boys and Girls schools. Boys of the HBL School wore long blue shirts, white *kufiya* and black *aqu'als*.

Boys from the military school in Mukalla parade at the Sultan's palace ca 1960. The headdress is a white *imama* with black *aqal*. A dark blue *qamees* is worn with red sash and cummerbund. (Mrs Edith Gray)

HBL Bedouin Boys School performing gymnastics at Mukalla Palace Courtyard 2 December 1966. (Sultan Ghalib)

Qu'aiti Bedouin Boys School saluting the Sultan (Ghalib bin Awadh al Qu'aiti II) who is seated next to the Resident Jim Ellis on the extreme right, 2 December 1962. (Sultan Ghalib)

H.H. Sultan Ghalib al Qu'aiti II reviews a parade by Boys of the HBL School (in blue shirts, white *kufiya* and black *aqu'als*), and the State's Bedouin Boys School (in khaki *kufiya*, black *aqu'al*, white shirts and khaki shorts). It was generally assumed that they were good enough to participate in the Earl's Court Tournament and there were serious plans about sending them to London for the purpose. However, political events were to intervene. (Sultan Ghalib)

During the 1960s Col. Eric Johnson and Col. Hillman considered sending the HBL boys to Earls Court to perform gymnastics in the Royal Tournament. This did not take place due to political events in South Arabia overtaking normal activities. Both HBL schools had a very good reputation and were very useful educational institutions, which were not just military in nature. Many of the students went on to lead non-military lives as *Madrasat abna' al badiyah*, or Sons of the Bedouins School, and *Madrassat banat al Badiyah*, or Daughters of the Bedouin School. These two schools also had a very good reputation for providing skills to the students as well as an education. Boys wore khaki *kufiya*, black *aqu'al*, white shirts and khaki shorts. The Bedouin Boy's School dates from the late 1930s and early 1940s.

VEHICLES AND WEAPONS

Photographs show from the early 1960s HBL vehicles were marked with a red line across the bonnet as an aid in identification, particularly by air, and a white HBL badge was painted on vehicle doors. Bedford RL lorries had the cab roof painted white. Red tactical sign plates were placed at the front and back of vehicles. These had a white Arabic inscription stating Hadhrami Bedouin Legion. Later that decade the vehicles reverted to a more sombre British army green. A yellow-over-red tactical sign, identical to the British Armoured Corps, was later used.

Rifles issued to the HBL were originally Indian-made .303 SMLE No. 1 Mk IIIs, which were later replaced by the Rifle No. 4 Mk I. As with other Eastern Aden Protectorate forces, captured Italian weapons were used shortly after the end of the Second World War. These consisted of Italian Breda 6.5 mm light machine guns and Austrian Schwarzlose 8mm medium machine guns. Ammunition and belts were no longer available after 1952, and they were replaced by .303 Bren Guns.

Table 8: Commandants of the Hadhrami Bedouin Legion

Rais Barakat	1939–1947
Major Ghulam Haider	1947–1949
Qaid Naif al Faiz	1949–1955
Qaid Khalaf Qaftan	1955–1957
Lt. Col. I.E. Snell	1957–1960
Lt. Col. J.W.G. Gray	1960–1966
Col. E.F. Johnson	1966–1967

Typical HBL fort in the Eastern Aden Protectorate. A red and white HBL flag is flying bearing the Legion's insignia in its centre. (Mrs Edith Gray)

HBL convoy in the interior ca 1960. All vehicles carry a red band over the vehicles bonnet, while RL Bedford 3-ton lorries also have a white roof enabling easy identification from the air. (Mrs Edith Gray)

HBL infantry up-country, ca 1960. The soldiers in this section are carrying No. 4 Mk I rifles.(Mrs Edith Gray)

IMAD LEVY

Imad was an Arab village a few miles along the coast east of Aden. In December 1915 a small levy of 100 men was raised to protect the village and to provide intelligence and guides for the British forces fighting in the Aden hinterland. The levy was officered by British and Indian soldiers. In his 'Report on the Operations of the Aden Field Force of 1st April – 18th August 1917' the GOC Aden states that on 9 April 1917 cavalry and infantry scouts sniped Jabir in the morning. In the afternoon some Somalis at Jabir attempted a reprisal on Imadis cutting wood in 'no man's land'. Their attack was repulsed by the Imad Levy. The Imad Levy grew in size and was later known as the Arab Levy. The authors note that the Arab Levy may in fact be the same as the Arab Legion mentioned in 1st Yemen Infantry.

KATHIRI ARMED CONSTABULARY

AL SHURTAH AL MASALLIHA AL KATHIRIYYAH

The Kathiri Sultans were descended from Badr Abu Tuwairiq, who led the Kathiri tribe from the High Yemen into the Hadhramaut during the latter part of the fifteenth century. They proceeded to overrun the area and ruled after the fashion of the times. They built up a tribal confederation, known as the Shanafir, around them. To support their rule they employed mercenary Yafa'is soldiers from the mountains of north-east Aden. In the latter part of the sixteenth century a group of these mercenaries, led by members of

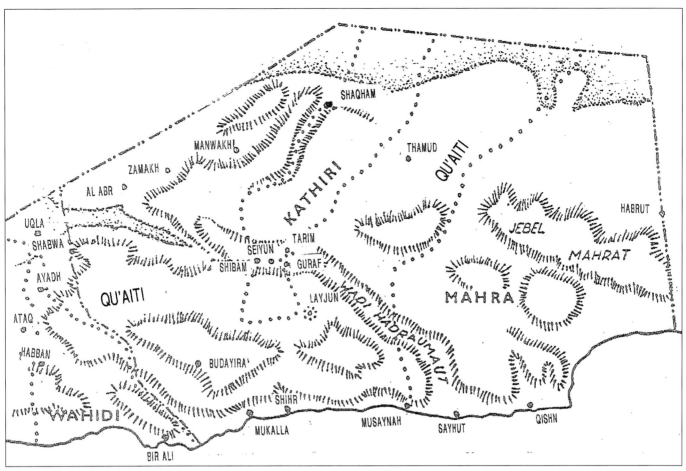

Eastern Aden Protectorate. (Cliff Lord)

Katheri Armed Constabulary ca 1939. (David Birtles)

the feud in Hyderabad, to the annoyance and disquiet of the Nizam. As the Qu'aiti had been in India longer, and had acquired more friends at court, the Kathiri was obliged to depart, and went home to make life difficult for the Qu'aiti in Hadhramaut.

By 1880, Kathiri State had lost much of its territory to Qu'aiti after a series of disastrous wars. The Kathiri Sultan found his African slaves more reliable administrators than his fellow tribesmen so that the descendants of the Sultan's slave army formed the majority of a force of about 80 tribal guard in 1939. Harold Ingrams had proposed the force several years earlier, and Captain R.A.B. Hamilton was tasked with raising the Kathiri Armed Constabulary (KAC) funded by a British government subsidy and the Kathiri State. Britain also supplied rifles and ammunition. The force was inspected by a British officer and trained by Arab instructors, and gradually the African element was replaced by tribesmen. In 1940 the KAC consisted of two officers, four *arif* and 61 *askers*.

During the Bin Abdat crises of the 1940s the KAC was too small in numbers to cope with the opposition, and support had to be brought in from Qu'aiti and Hyderabad to deal with the

the small Qu'aiti sub-tribe, seized the area of Al Qatn, which had the best agricultural land in the Hadhramaut, and established their own rule there. Consequently, a series of wars between the Kathiri and the Qu'aiti ensued, and over the next 300 years most towns changed hands at least twice. Many Hadhrami travelled abroad to India and the Far East to trade or to serve as mercenary soldiers. About 1840 the two most successful Arab mercenary soldiers in India were Umar Bin Awadh al Qu'aiti and Ghalib bin Mohsin al Kathiri, who each commanded a regiment in the army of the Nizam of Hyderabad. At feud in Hadhramaut, they continued

problem. After the crisis was resolved the KAC maintained a fair degree of peace and quiet via small outposts and a reserve at Husn Howarith, on the eastern outskirts of Seiyun. Within the confines of a small State, and possessing a good commander, Saleh al Jabri – an NCO transferred from the HBL and commissioned – the Kathiri State became a fairly peaceful place until independence. *Rais* Saleh Bin Sala'an, a senior officer in the KAC, was never fully trusted by the Sultan and his family as conveyed to Sultan Ghalib Al-Qu'aiti on a number of occasions. However, at the time of the NLF take-over, he proved his loyalty by taking to the hills and attempted to organise resistance. He was to die naturally while in the hills.

The Kathiri were originally armed with the French Le Gras rifle, known in the Hadhramaut as *Hotfa*. These used lead bullets and black powder cartridges. They were replaced by Italian 6.5 mm rifles and Austrian 8mm cavalry carbines captured in Eritrea during the Second World War. During the 1950s these weapons were replaced with British .303 Rifles, SMLE No. 1 Mk III, manufactured in India during the Second World War.

The KAC wore a khaki drill shirt and shorts, with a brown leather belt. KAC headdress consisted of a dark green *imama* with black *aqu'al*. No cap badge was ever made, but the constabulary wore a straight metal shoulder title with Arabic script. Boots were not worn.

LAHEJ POLICE

SHURTAT LAHIJ

Lahej possessed its own police force, which included a traffic police section, and responsibility for the prison. Police uniform consisted of a khaki drill tunic and trousers, dark blue putties worn up to the knee and *chaplis*. The black leather belt that was worn had a large metal buckle similar in size to that of the Aden Police. The traffic police wore white sleeves. Lahej police were quite distinctive in that they had their own unique headdress, which was a khaki pith helmet with khaki cloth flap covering the neck. This style of helmet was very similar to that worn by police in Jordan, but without the spike on top. A metal hat badge was fixed in the front, which was of a similar shape and size to the Aden Police cap badge. The badge had the inscription in Arabic: SULTANATE OF LAHEJ POLICE LAHEJ POLICE.

LAHEJ TRAINED FORCES

KUWWAT LAHIJ

Lahej was the largest city in the Western Aden Protectorate, and in many respects mirrored Mukalla in the Eastern Aden Protectorate as the pre-eminent seat of control for that area. A British Political Officer resided there, but Lahej never possessed the same importance, from a

Lahej Policeman, 1963. The headdress is similar to a Jordanian Police helmet but without a spike on top. A Sultanate of Lahej Police cap badge is worn on its front. (Michael Crouch)

Table 9: Composition of the Lahej Trained Forces in September 1940

	Officers	Other Ranks
Headquarters	3	6
One 10-pdr Gun Section	1	23
One MG Troop	2	56
Seven Infantry Platoons	5	220
Wireless Personnel		17
Band		26
Detachments		
Ras Ara		1 Platoon less one section 1 W/T Detachment
Khor Umera		1 Section
Tor Al Baha		2 Sections (inc. one Lewis Gun)
Kursh		1 Section 1 W/T Detachment
Transport		
MT, Dodge Trucks, 2		for MGs
Mules, 16		for Lewis Guns and SAA
Camels, 8		for 10-pdr Section
Camels, 6		for MG Section
Five trucks were also available for military use which were owned by H.H. the Sultan		
Arms		
300 SMLE rifles (new)		
4 Vickers Guns		
8 Lewis Guns		
2 10-pdr BL Mountain Guns (old but serviceable)		

colonial perspective, as Mukalla did. The Lahej Trained Force was founded after the First World War.

A report on the Lahej Trained Forces in September 1940 by Lt Col J G Worth Inspector General Lahej Trained Forces and Commander of the APL shows the composition of the force commanded by Sultan Salih bin Mehdi.

IRREGULARS

The Sultan had an irregular Camel patrol of about 40 men armed with Long Lee-Enfield Rifles and two Vickers-Berthier machine guns, which were under control of Abid Al Muntissor MBE. A considerable number of other arms of various makes and age were issued to tribesmen. These included Long Lee-Enfield, Martini-Henry, French and Turkish rifles.

ARTILLERY

The Artillery were well trained and carried out their gun drill with precision. Two men were trained and proficient in the use of the Barr and Stroud rangefinder.

VICKERS MACHINE GUNS

Two Dodge trucks were fitted identically to those in use in the APL. One Vickers machine gun was placed on each, and two were to remain with the infantry companies.

INFANTRY

The Infantry consisted of two companies of three sections and a reserve section. A good standard of drill and weapon training existed.

WIRELESS

The Lahej Trained Forces had efficient operators, but some difficulty was experienced in obtaining valves, battery and other replacements. The wireless sets came under the Signals Officer Khormaksar Station for general supervision.

BAND

The band was to be trained in Stretcher drill and First Aid.

EQUIPMENT

Personal Equipment locally made was to replace older mixed equipment.

A detachment of Lahej Trained Forces (LTF) were sent to assist in guard duties in Aden while the APL was training during November and December 1940. They were reported to be exemplary in their duties. By the late 1950s the LTF was sometimes referred to as the Lahej Regular Army (LRA). Following a visit to Scotland the Sultan introduced a pipe band, which became highly sought-after in Aden for functions. In 1957 the entire band accompanied the Sultan and a large number of the LTF into Yemen to escape internal feuding within the State. The Commandant of the APL was 'ex-officio' Inspector General of the LTF.

UNIFORM

By the late 1930s the Lahej Trained Forces (LTF) wore a uniform of khaki shirt, shorts and *pagri*. No specific headdress badge or metal shoulder titles were ever produced. The uniform remained similar into the 1950s, but the khaki *pagri* had a red flash with a white bar and a fringe worn on the left-hand side and was similar in style to the APL green and white flash. The significance, perhaps taken

from the flag of Lahej, was in red and white. After 1956, a khaki beret replaced the *pagri*. British Army rank insignia was worn.

LAHEJ TRIBAL GUARDS

Lahej had its own Tribal Guards which were raised in the late forties. (See Tribal Guard)

MAHRA TRIBAL GUARD

AL HARAS AL QABALI AL MAHRI

Mahra was the last State in the Protectorates to be pacified. Located in the east of the Eastern Aden Protectorate, Mahra was a lawless tract of land remote from civilisation. A treaty had been signed with the Sultan, who resided on the island of Socotra. In theory the State was a part of the Eastern Aden Protectorate. In reality it contained many tribes who refused to accept the Sultan's authority, and, for example, there were Kathiri tribesmen who had been feuding with the Mahra for almost four centuries. Consequently, the treaty with the British was a worthless piece of paper. The British turned a blind eye to the problem as it was not worth the cost of a major expedition until oil companies showed an interest in the area.

It was not until the early 1960s that the Hadhrami Bedouin Legion was called upon to show a presence in the State and establish a number of small forts there. This was done with some skill and daring, and, as a consequence, a small Mahra Tribal Guard (MTG) was established in 1965. This was similar in structure to the former Tribal Guards of the Western Aden Protectorate, who had been merged with the Government Guard into FNG2 in 1959. The Mahra were never considered for membership of the Federation. The Colonial Office subsidised the Mahra State, and the bulk of the Mahra Tribal Guard's money came from that subsidy. Little is known of the unit, other than that the soldiers were uniformed in the usual khaki drill shirt and shorts and had the distinction of wearing a black and white *imama* headdress with *aqu'al*.

MILITARY ASSISTANT TO THE RESIDENT ADVISER (MARA), EASTERN ADEN PROTECTORATE

MASA'ID AL MUSTASHAR AL HARBI

Unlike the Western Aden Protectorate, which was close to Aden Colony and consequently to support from political and military forces, the Eastern Aden Protectorate was remote and difficult to reach, except by air. The eastern States also had to be aware of the ever-present threat from Saudi Arabia. Nevertheless, most of its difficulties were internal. Harold Ingrams, the first Resident Adviser, recognised the unique difficulties of his domain. Accordingly, he established the post of Military Assistant to the Resident Adviser (MARA), aimed at raising the standard of training of the various military and paramilitary forces of the Protectorate, in particular of the newly raised Hadhrami Bedouin Legion. A number of very experienced and capable officers served in this post until 1967. The Military Assistant was tasked with ensuring that all of the various military forces in the Eastern Aden Protectorate received sufficient training, and that these units were up to the standards required. Because of his close liaison with the different military groups, it was only natural that he was able to co-ordinate the movement of all of the forces in that Protectorate. He had a well-trained and disciplined – albeit somewhat diverse – force at his disposal, which was attuned to the needs of every corner of the Protectorate except Mahra State, which was not pacified until the 1960s. The combination of stable military force, good colonial administration, fewer sheikhdoms and sultanates, and its geographical location, meant that the Eastern Aden Protectorate was more peaceful and more autonomous than the Western Aden Protectorate. This was reflected in the fact that none of the eastern States (with the exception of Wahidi) were to join the Federation.

MUKALLA PRISON POLICE

AL SHURTAH LI'L SUJOON B'IL MUKALLA

In Qu'aiti State there were a number of Armed Constabulary lockups, but only one prison, which was situated in Mukalla. The prison was well-run and organised, but the accommodation is reported to have been basic. In 1940 the Prison establishment comprised a Chief Warden and 13 Wardens. Shihr had 10 Wardens. Prison police wore a curved brass shoulder title, which bore the Arabic inscription SHURTAH LI'L SUJOON B'IL MUKALLA, which translates as Mukalla Prison Police. This title was first issued in 1964. The khaki uniform was similar to the Civil Police except they wore a black *pagri* and wore a black *usra* or cummerbund on ceremonial occasions.

MUKALLA REGULAR ARMY

JAISH AL MUKALLA AL NIDHAMI

By far the largest and most developed State in the Eastern Aden Protectorate was the Qu'aiti Sultanate of Shihr and Mukalla. The Sultan, who resided in the city of Mukalla, was also hereditary commander of a large body of Arab irregular troops in the service of the Nizam of Hyderabad, the largest native State in India. His estates in Hyderabad were lucrative and helped to shore up the shakier finances of his State in Arabia. The Qu'aiti State's troops (regular and irregular tribal levies) had existed since the dynasty's attempts to establish an independent kingdom. However, the title 'Mukalla Regular Army' (MRA) had formally come into being in the late 1930s. The Qu'aiti army had at stages even included some Indians, particularly Rohillas (Indian-Afghans). They were replaced by Arabs upon their arrival in Hyderabad, chiefly by bribing the authorities. These Rohillas in the Qu'aiti army mostly served specific functions involving regular training. For example, they were gunners from the mid-nineteenth century, when they waged a protracted, but successful war with the Kathiris and others. An early mention of the army is to be found in The Historical Record of the Imperial Visit to India 1911, which records that the Sultan of Shehr and Mokalla was escorted by a body of horsemen in red and white uniforms. During the 1930s the State possessed a trained military force of some 400 men, mainly Yafa'i tribesmen and the descendants of African slaves, plus about 1,000 or more irregular tribesmen. The officers were Indian, although they drilled in English. On ceremonial parades they wore blue and gold laced tunics, red breeches with a broad blue stripe, and squat *tarbooshes*, as did the State's band.

By 1940 the MRA consisted of:

Infantry
Three Companies of eight platoons, with three Sections to each Platoon
The composition of the platoons was:
3 Platoons of Hadhrami tribesmen
1 Platoon of Jebel *Yafai*

1 Platoon of *Thelud* (implying Hadhrami born) Yafai
3 Platoons of Slaves

Garrisons were located at Mukalla, Gheil-Ba-Wazir and Shihr. They also provided Expeditionary Forces. Troops were also located at Gheil bin Yumain, Al 'Abr, and Bir 'Asakir.
MRA Establishment in 1940 was a total 276 all ranks.

HIS HIGHNESS' BODYGUARD AND MACHINE GUN SECTION
The MRA also included His Highness' Bodyguard and Machine Gun Section. Their duties were to provide bodyguard patrols and armament consisted of lances; Rifles SMLE, and machine guns.

CAMEL TROOP
Mounted on camels and armed with lances the ceremonial Camel Troop wore a uniform of dark blue *pagri* with light blue horizontal stripes wrapped around a dark blue *khulla*, red tunics, dark blue shorts, dark blue cummerbunds and dark blue putties and sandals. They were mainly recruited from a branch of the Nahdi Tribal Confederation. The pennant on the lance was red over white. The Camel Troop was a quasi-independent section of the MRA and consisted of a *Resaldar* and 11 Troopers.

SULTAN'S EQUERRIES, ADC AND BODYGUARD
The Sultan's equerries, ADC and bodyguard were quasi-independent MRA members although Major Salem Abdullah al Fardi had last been in charge of the Coast Guard Police before his transfer to the palace as Sultan Ghalib's last equerry.

SULTAN'S ARMED SLAVES
There was an establishment of 461 African armed slaves within the Sultan's force in 1940, issued with miscellaneous rifles.

MRA ARTILLERY BATTERY
Captain Sheppard inspected the MRA in 1940, and his investigation of the artillery resources of the Mukalla Government discovered a great deal of material. This included artillery from almost every period in history. There were bronze guns, iron guns, many casks of gunpowder in good condition and a vast assortment of cannon balls in mint condition. Also, there was chain-shot and grape-shot, muskets, primers and powder flasks, still wrapped in paper. There

Fairey F3 preparing to take a local ruler on a flight. Early 1930s. (Frank Edwards)

The Qu'aiti Armed Forces on parade in the palace courtyard Mukalla circa 1947. The Camel Troop of the Qu'aiti Sultanic Guard (MRA) dressed in dark blue *pagri* with light blue stripes wrapped around a dark blue kulah, (vertical stripes), wearing red tunics, dark blue shorts, dark blue cummerbunds, dark blue putties and local sandals. The Troop was armed with lances. They were mostly recruited from a branch of the Nahdi Tribal Confederation. (Sultan Ghalib)

The Qu'aiti Armed Forces on parade circa 1947 in the courtyard of the Sultan's main residential palace at Mukalla. The light mountain battery guns were acquired from HM Government by Sultan Ghalib I. The ceremonial Camel Troop was a part of the Sultan's processional guard. (Sultan Ghalib)

The MRA post at Qa'udha, seat of one of the three paramount chiefs of the Nahdi Tribal Confederation, being inspected by the Amir Ghalib al Qu'aiti during 1961. A 3-inch mortar can be seen centrally. (Sultan Ghalib)

Qu'aiti military post at Qa'udha. The young heir apparent Amir Ghalib al Qu'aiti and his younger brother Amir 'Omar inspecting a guard of honour of the MRA. (Sultan Ghalib)

were cannon ball bombs still in their boxes in which they were issued and with a great quantity of fuse. Further to this there were muzzle loading seven pounder guns, two 10-pounder guns with a great deal of ancillary equipment and about 800 shells complete with fuses, cordite and other items and three 7-pounder guns. One 2.75-inch gun with 100 rounds of HE was due to arrive late February 1941.

The Officer Commanding the Artillery Section wore a *tarboosh*, Khaki shirt, Shin long shorts, golfing stockings and tennis shoes. The duties of the Artillery Section were ceremonial and expeditions. The section was issued with Martini-Henry Rifles. 1 officer 5 NCOs and 29 Men.

After the Second World War, the Artillery Section consisted of two 2.75-inch mountain guns. They were known as 'pip-squeaks' and were capable of blowing holes in most of the mud forts of up-country malcontents. These guns, which could be carried by camel and quickly assembled, lasted until 1955. They were then replaced by a 2-pdr anti-tank gun which could be towed by a Land Rover.

BAND

Within the MRA in the 1940s there were three Bands, although not as professional even during the days of Sultan Awadh bin 'Umar as the Qu'aiti State Band. They were locally known as the

'Trumpetah' and played during the inspecting of troops and at minor functions. The bands had their own budget and command structure and was located separately from the MRA barracks.

They consisted of:

Indian Band – although called the Indian Band it comprised 21 Arab and Somali musicians
Arab Band – there were eight Arab and five slave musicians
Shihr Band – entirely slaves

IRREGULARS

This group consisted of 12 Muqaddams and 600 men.

Of the many different sections within the MRA only the band and infantry survived until 1967. While on active service, camels

The Mukalla Sultanic Band ca 1964. They wore white *pagri*, white ceremonial dress and black shoes. They are followed by a company of MRA distinguished by the rank and file's red *pagri* for parades, replacing the normal khaki *pagri*. (Jim Ellis)

and often donkeys were hired for activities in country inaccessible to motor transport. Until the 1930s armament was mainly the Martini-Henry, a single-shot, lever-action, breech-loading weapon firing .455" lead bullets with black powder cartridges. These were later replaced by Indian-produced SMLE .303 rifles. During 1938 Colonel Robinson of the APL spent some time with the MRA and put them on a sound footing. After the Second World War further rearmament occurred, using weapons captured from the Italians in Ethiopia, Eritrea and Somaliland. Breda 6.5mm light machine guns, and ex-Austrian 8mm carbines and Schwarzlose medium machine guns were available. The Austrian weapons had been captured by the Italians in 1918. After the ammunition ran out the MRA were re-armed with No. 4 Rifles and Brens. A proportion of the force was always on duty in small groups in distant parts of the State, cooperating closely with the British-paid Hadhrami Bedouin Legion. This force had been patterned on the Trans-Jordanian Arab Legion's 'Desert Patrol'. It was originally conceived as a force around a company strong, with the aim of promoting the trust of the Bedouins in the Government's reforms. Its strength until the dawn of the 1960s was just three companies, and later on four. Only after 1965 was its strength doubled to seven or eight companies and it was only to begin to play a greater role in international frontier patrolling alongside the State's troops from the 1950s, while valuable assets were reallocated by the State to other fields like education, health and roadbuilding, as the HBL was completely financed by the British Residency and was to remain under their command. The tactics of the two forces remained very similar.

With independence the *Yafa'i* element drifted away, usually taking their arms with them. Many found their way to the Persian Gulf (now the Arabian Gulf to the Arabs) and enlisted in the forces of the Emirates. As long as Qaid Saleh bin Someida' commanded the MRA they remained effective. However, in 1966 he was promoted to the command of all Qu'aiti forces. His successor, a *Yafa'i* named Qaid Ahmed al Yezidi, did not possess the same drive or charisma, and as a consequence the reliability of the MRA became suspect. In 1967 this became rather obvious when an NLF-inspired mob broke into the British Residency compound, forcing the HBL to fire over their heads to disperse them. The MRA guard in the Sultan's palace opposite fired on the upper floors of the Residency until the Sultan personally intervened. Following its abandonment by the British, independence soon came to the Eastern Aden Protectorate. When the Qu'aiti and Kathiri Sultans were both in Geneva at the behest of the British and the United Nations the small British presence was withdrawn. Bin Someid'a and the Governor of Mukalla, Badr al Kasadi held the remains of the Qu'aiti administration together until overwhelmed by the National Liberation Front, who imprisoned both along with others who opposed them. While in prison, these two kept the spirits of the other prisoners up until an exasperated NLF executed them.

UNIFORM

The uniform of the *Yafi'i* tribesmen in the 1930s, whom Philby in his book *Sheba's Daughters* states were from the Sultan's own clan and had been trained by Colonel Lake and other British officers in the Aden Levy or the Yemen Infantry, is described simply as khaki shorts and shirts. The Sultan's slaves were in uniforms of red and blue with a liberal sprinkling of gold braid. There were also a squad of cadets and a band.

The sealed pattern Crown Agents headdress in 1939 consisted of:

Kullah, blue drill
Pagri, Khaki Cotton
Pagri, red cotton

During the Second World War the red and blue uniforms of the MRA were discarded for khaki shirts and shorts with locally made leather equipment. For ceremonial parades a red Indian-style *pagri* replaced the work dress khaki *pagri*, and a red cummerbund was worn under the brown leather belt. The red was a link to the earlier uniforms and to that of the Arab Regiment in Hyderabad. No footwear was worn. While on garrison duty officers wore a British-style black field service hat with red piping, crown and peak. Other ranks had a plain khaki field service hat with a red peak. On parade officers wore khaki Indian-style *pagri* with *shamla*, shirts, trousers, Sam Browne, sword and tan shoes. While attached to the HBL the gunners had the distinction of wearing the Hadhrami Bedouin Legion *imama* and *aqu'al*. The MRA did not have its own cap badge, but all ranks wore brass shoulder titles. Designed by Sultan Saleh bin Ghalib, these were worn from 1947. A shoulder title for the band was introduced in 1960. British rank

MRA Guard of Honour for Lord Beswick who is escorted by a HBL officer, 1965. (Sultan Ghalib)

Sultan Ghalib of Mukalla with his ADC, 1960s. (Owain Raw-Rees)

MRA on parade at the Sultan's palace. Officers wear a khaki tunic, *pagri* with *shamla* and shorts. Other Ranks wear khaki uniforms with red *pagri* and cummerbund, the latter beneath a leather belt. (Jim Ellis)

The Amir 'Awadh bin Saleh al Qu'aiti (Heir Apparent) on board a visiting Royal Navy warship with Resident Adviser Colonel Hugh Boustead, ca 1954. (Sultan Ghalib)

The Amir Muhammed bin Ghalib, the second son of Sultan Ghalib al Qu'aiti I, who was to pass away in youth. He is dressed in a green blue tunic laced with gold. The breeches were red with gold stripes and a Qu'aiti style turban wrapped around a fez. This was the ceremonial attire of Qu'aiti troops for display purposes up to the 1940s, ca 1890s. (Sultan Ghalib)

H.H. Sultan 'Omar bin 'Awadh al Qu'aiti (reigned 1922–1936) following his elder brother Ghalib bin 'Awadh I (reined 1910–1922). The medals worn are the 1903 and 1911 Delhi Durbar medals. Below the medals is a diamond star of his own design and choice. He had made an official visit to Lahej on this occasion as a guest of H.H. Sultan 'Abdul-Kareem Fadhl al 'Abdali. Circa 1930 in Aden. (Sultan Ghalib)

insignia was worn by all Eastern Aden Protectorate forces. Sultan Ghalib opines that the buttons on his first uniform were crossed *jambias* initially, but after that his brother Omar had new buttons introduced with a castle surrounded by oak leaves with the legend, in a white metal circle, 'Al-Quwwat Al-Qu'aitiyya Al-Musalliha' in Arabic and 'Qu'aiti Armed Forces' in English.

The Commanding Officer of the MRA delivers a speech during the early 1960s. (Jim Ellis)

December 1966 – The MRA HQ and parade and training ground outside Mukalla known locally as 'Regiment'. Girls from a school for the daughters of soldiers present H.H. Sultan Ghalib al Qu'aiti II with a memento made by them. They are accompanied by Saleh Rubaiyya' al Jabri, a medical orderly in the MRA. (Sultan Ghalib)

H.H. Sultan 'Omar al Qu'aiti touring his provinces of the Sultanate in 1934. Left to right; one of the Nidham (slave regulars); the Sultan on horseback; his constant equerry and bodyguard Saleh 'Ali al Khulaqi; and a *nidhami* (formally trained troops). (Sultan Ghalib)

Lord Beswick's Visit. November 1965 at the British Residency, Mukalla. Left to right; John Ducker (Assistant to the Resident Adviser); Lord Beswick Vincent Eyre (British Agent and Resident Adviser).
Those on parade, left to right; Maj. Gen. Saleh Yislam Bin Sumaida' (Military Secretary to the Wazir); Major Mohsin al Marfadi (CO of the Prison Guard); Lt Col Nasser 'Awadh al Batati (CO of the QAC); Lt Col Ahmed 'Abdullah al Yazeedi (CO of the MRA); Lt Col Ahmed Abdullah Effendi (CO of the Customs Police and Coast Guard); Lt Col Ahmed Bin Muneef (CO of the Civil Police); Major David Eales (HBL). (Sultan Ghalib)

Mukalla palace throne room 1 December 1966. H.H. Sultan Ghalib al Qu'aiti II receiving guests on the morning of his official investiture. Behind him stands his bodyguard Corporal (later Sergeant) Muhsin 'Omar al- Muflehi and next to him Captain Rubaiyya' al Jabri (MRA) – Equerry. On the extreme left is Mr Young a senior political officer for the South Arabian Federation. (Sultan Ghalib)

The Amir 'Awadh bin Saleh al Qu'aiti (Heir Apparent) on board a visiting Royal Navy warship with Resident Adviser Colonel Hugh Boustead, ca 1954. (Sultan Ghalib)

H.H. Sultan Ghalib al Qu'aiti II, November 1966. The service uniform is in khaki with an olive green beret. The metal headdress badge is a gold-coloured crossed swords encompassed with a wreath, which had been designed by Amir Umar. The badge was held in place with a pin fitting. (Sultan Ghalib)

H.H. Sultan 'Omar bin 'Awadh al Qu'aiti (reigned 1922–1936) dressed in a uniform for an Imperial Assemblage in India – probably the 1911 Durbar in Delhi. (Sultan Ghalib)

H.H. Sultan Sir Ghalib bin 'Awadh al Qu'aiti in uniform after receiving the KCIE. (Sultan Ghalib)

Table 11: Qu'aiti Sultans

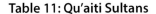

Sultan Ghalib wearing a green beret and gorget tabs. The cap badge is of the Sultans brother's design. (Sultan Ghalib)

Uniform designed by H.H. Sultan Ghalib al Qu'aiti II for himself in 1966 as a "Musheer" or Marshal of the Qu'aiti Armed Forces. The rank, recommended by Colonel Eric Johnson, was meant to imply the head of the armed forces. It would have been higher than the rank of "Liwa'" (Major General) held by "al-Sekrtayr al Harbi" (Military Secretary – though the actual translation would be Secretary of State for War) held by Yislam Saleh Bin Sumaida'. (Sultan Ghalib)

H.H. Sultan Ghalib Bin Awadh Al-Qu'aiti II dressed to visit HMS *Kedleston*, a minesweeper off al Mukalla, 2 December 1966. (Sultan Ghalib)

Right to Left: Prince Saleh bin Ghalib (later Sultan 1936–1956) and his younger brother Muhammad bin Ghalib in Bombay, possibly prior to the great Imperial Durbar of 1902–3 at Delhi. The latter, a crack shot and horseman was shortly to die of mysterious circumstances, possibly asphyxiation! Between them stands the family's representative and agent in Bombay, 'AbdAllah bin Muhsin Bubak al-Haddadi (al Qu'aiti). (Sultan Ghalib)

Table 10: Qu'aiti Armed Forces Ranks

Rank	Equivalent
Musheer	'Marshal' (not Field-Marshal) implying Commander-in-Chief (The Sultan)
Liwa	Major General
Aqid	Colonel
Qaid	Lieutenant Colonel
Wakil Qaid	Major
Rais	Captain
Mulazim Awal	Lieutenant
Mulazim Thani	Second Lieutenant
Naqib	Sergeant (note that there was no Staff Sergeant rank)
Areef	Corporal
Wakil Areef	Lance Corporal
Jundi	Private
Jundi Murash'shah	Officer Cadet
Shabit	Cadet

A parade in Mukalla about 1947. An HBL orderly is standing by the car while Mukalla Civil Police in their dark blue uniforms and *tarboosh* may be seen in the background. With the Camel Troop on the right is Lad Khan, formerly of the Indian Army, the Commanding officer of the MRA. (Sultan Ghalib)

Sultanic Guard, ca 1929. (David Birtles)

The Mukalla Palace Courtyard, 1 December 1966. H.H. Sultan Ghalib Al Qu'aiti II reviews a parade by Boys of the HBL and State schools. (Sultan Ghalib)

'Umar I	1865
'Awadh I	1866–1909
Ghalib I	1909–1922
'Umar II	1922–1936
Saleh	1936–1956
Awadh II	1956–1966
Ghalib II	1966 to present

QU'AITI ARMED CONSTABULARY

AL SHURTAH AL-MUSALLIHA AL-QU'AITIYYA

IRREGULARS

During the early twentieth century the Qu'aiti Sultan maintained a force of *Yafa'i* irregulars in the settled areas along the coast, and in those parts of the Hadhramaut which gave allegiance to him. The Constabulary was housed in forts or fortified houses in or near towns and villages and at the disposal of the *Na'ib* (Governor), or the *Qa'im* (District Commissioner). They were paid a retainer and allowed the privilege of private trade. Their duties included delivering summonses, supervising punishments and collecting fines and taxes. The soldiers were usually recruited from the mountains north-east of Aden. In the early days the Qu'aiti Armed Constabulary were armed with the French Le Gras rifle, known as '*Hotfa*'. The black powder was made locally, as were the bullets, mainly at *Shihr*. Rifles too, were repaired there under government's sponsorship on the scale of a cottage industry, but this was to come to an end before the second decade of the twentieth century.

GENDARMERIE

In 1937 courses were started in *Shihr* to upgrade younger irregulars and new recruits from nearby tribes into a cohesive uniformed force called the Gendarmerie. They were still armed with the Le Gras rifle, but some tribesmen had succeeded in acquiring more modern rifles, either .303 Lee-Enfield's (some marked '*Feisal*' which had been issued to the Army of the Hejaz in World War I) or 7.92mm Mausers. In 1940 the Gendarmerie comprised 150 all ranks in 10 *firqas*.

The Qu'aiti Gendarmerie ('Gendarma') in *futah* at al-Shihr. The *futah* was a multi-coloured kilt locally woven in al-Shihr, worn before the transformation of this force into the Qu'aiti Armed Constabulary (QAC). The QAC was the largest force in the State. In the background is the old fort Husn Bin 'Ayyash which had been rebuilt during the late 1860 and 1870s but left unfinished. The strength of its walls had been tested with cannon fire before final approval. (Sultan Ghalib)

QU'AITI ARMED CONSTABULARY

The Qu'aiti Armed Constabulary (QAC) was formed about 1949, in replacement of the Gendarmerie, but incorporating its manpower. The new force was paid for by the Qu'aiti State and was similar to a rural police force, but armed. The Military Assistant to the Resident Adviser of the Eastern Aden Protectorate, Major Jock Snell, upgraded the new force by arming them with Indian-made .303 Rifles, SMLE No. 1 Mk III. Recruits increasingly came from within the State rather than from Yafa'i. Their last commander was Qaid Nasir Awadh al Batati, a Yafa'i born in Java but brought up in Hadhramaut. He ran the training depot outside the city of Mukalla and acted as inspector to the individual provincial forces which served the provinces, their districts, towns and villages of Shihr, Shibam, Duan, Hajr and later on the newly created Western Province with its capital at Haura, as well as the rural areas of Mukalla. Each province possessed a commanding officer of the rank of a *rais* (captain). From time to time the officer, NCOs and men were transferred regularly between provinces or to and from headquarters as a matter of policy after the reforms. Jim Ellis, the last Resident Adviser in the Eastern Aden Protectorate, recalls that their effectiveness greatly depended upon how well the provincial governors (Naibs) and District Officers (Qaims) used them. However, they were generally reliable and far superior to any similar force outside Aden. Many of the force were absorbed successfully into the so-called People's Army following independence.

EMERGENCY ROAD GUARDS

This unit was functionally a Gendarmerie paid for by the Mukalla Government and was recommended by Captain Sheppard, who inspected the unit, that it should be merged with the Qu'aiti Gendarmerie. The purpose of this unit was to provide protection for the caravan routes – 'al-Tariq al-Qibli' (West Road), from Mukalla to Hadhramaut's Interior and 'al-Tariq al-Sharqi' (the East Road) from Shihr to Wadi Hadhramaut. This unit boasted of 116 all ranks in 1940 and had initially two lorries, which increased with each company at least possessing one, this in addition to other lorries and tankers belonging to the transport unit. No further details have been found and it is supposed that this unit became absorbed into the QAC.

AL-KAF ROAD PATROL

One *chaoush* and four *sowars*. Their function was to deal with minor incidents on the Al-Kaf road. They provided their own camels.

QAC UNIFORM

The State issued *Futahs* and *Pagri* (wrapped around the head in indigenous style as opposed to cockscomb); but only for two of the 10 Firqas in 1940. The QAC initially had their own silver headdress badge locally made and wore dark blue putties and *tarboosh* until the 1950s. Later the QAC uniform comprised a khaki shirt and shorts and brown leather belt. Headdress consisted of a khaki *imama* with black *aqu'al*. A red lanyard was worn on the left shoulder and had a whistle attached. Other ranks had no footwear. No cap badge was worn, but in 1958 a curved brass shoulder title was issued, stamped with the wording 'ARMED CONSTABULARY' in Arabic. This was changed to 'QU'AITI ARMED CONSTABULARY' in 1962.

QU'AITI CIVIL POLICE

AL SHURTAH AL-MADANIYYAH

Town Police were raised in 1900 at *Shihr* and later at Mukalla. By the 1940s their uniform was dark blue with black *baghloos* (belt) with a white metal buckle, dark blue putties and thick Western style sandals and a dark blue *tarboosh*. A dark blue *usra* or cummerbund was worn on ceremonial occasions. The dark blue lanyard had a whistle attached. A specially made forage cap was introduced, possibly in the 1950s, which was khaki with the peak of the cap being black. About the same time black Bata sandals were issued. The police baton was black. Circa 1965, when under the command of Lt. Col. Ahmed Bin Muneef, new badges made in white metal were issued. There was a locally made white metal headdress badge, which was worn on the left side of the forage cap and in the centre of peak caps by officers. The design was a large castle in the centre and crossed batons or similar supporting it. Encompassing the badges were two branches of leaves and a scroll with the words AL SHURTAH AL-MADANIYYAH or Civil Police in Arabic. All ranks wore from that time a white metal shoulder title.

Ranks were uniform throughout State's forces and consisted of the following in 1940:

Commandant
Jamadar
Havildar
3 Naik
7 Lance Naik
53 Sepoys

The rank titles were later Arabised.

Eid Day after the prayers. Mukalla circa 1947. In the Sultan's absence, the State Secretary (Wazir) Sheikh Saif bin 'Ali al-Bu'ali, (a Zanzibari Omani) being escorted by the Sultan's Lancers, the Ceremonial Camel Troop. The Civil Police, in their traditional dark blue uniforms and *tarboosh*, surround the vehicle. The blue was changed later to khaki and the tarboush replaced by a forage cap. They also wore dark blue putties and cummerbunds and carried a baton after the fashion of the English 'Bobby'. (Sultan Ghalib)

Mukalla City Police hat showing the officers hat badge. (Sultan Ghalib)

The Town Police was actually the Qu'aiti Civil Police. This is reflected by their shoulder title. Al-Shihr Town Police was to be absorbed into the QAC, which had been expanded and all police duties came under them except for Mukalla.

QU'AITI CIVIL POLICE CUSTOMS SECTION

A khaki forage cap with a yellow peak distinguished them from the Civil Police and a yellow cummerbund was used on ceremonial occasions. Dark blue putties were worn. The Customs Section had their own metal shoulder title. In 1940 the section comprised 37 Customs and Harbour Police.

QU'AITI SULTANIC BAND

AL-JAGUAR AL-SULTANIYYAH

The Qu'aiti Sultanic Band was the State's band for all the forces in the State, and a group from them also performed at soirees. The band's HQ and facilities were at Sharij Ba Salim across the estuary from Mukalla. By 1965, the band had acquired a new ceremonial uniform after the departure of Lt. Col. Deswande Khan. He was replaced by Major Abdul Quader Jum'ah Khan. Prior to 1965, the uniform consisted of black sandals, white *pagri* and *khulla*, white tunics which buttoned up to the neck for bandsmen while the Bandmaster had a white shirt and black tie, white jacket and

The photograph shows the uniform of the Qu'aiti Sultanic Band up until the 1960s. Band Master, Major (Later Lt. Col.) Daswande Khan, wears a khaki uniform. Second from the left in white uniform is Capt. Abdul Qadir Jum'a Khan who was to take over from him. His family were originally Rohillas who specialised in gunnery and were brought over from India for operations in Hadhramaut and settled down there, ca 1960. (Sultan Ghalib)

Qu'aiti Sultanic Band in ceremonial uniform issued before 1965. (Sultan Ghalib)

trousers. At soirees they wore their white *pagri*, white tunic and sarong. The new uniform of 1965 was comprised of white tunics, black trousers with red stripes and forage caps in black with a red crown, front and gold piping. The Bandmaster wore a red sash and a black tie and carried an officer's ceremonial sword with a metal scabbard. Black shoes replaced the black sandals. The colour red was an inference to the Himyaritic roots of the Yafa'is and their old flag which was plain red. A working dress of black sandals, khaki tunic and long trousers and a khaki forage cap was also worn. The wearing of long trousers implied the band was more civilian as short trousers were considered military.

QU'AITI SULTANIC GUARD

FIRQAT HARAS ADHUMAT AL SULTAN AL KHAS

His Highness' Bodyguard and Machine Gun Section date back to the 1940s when the MRA was reorganised and modernised. The Camel Troop of Lancers was also a quasi-independent part of the MRA. These units were always affiliated to the MRA, if not always recruited from its ranks. The Machine Gun Section was reabsorbed into the MRA in the mid-1950s whereas the Camel Lancers faded away around 1956. With His Highness Sultan Ghalib II's accession in 1966 he chose a new design for a fresh uniform for QSG. The QSG was a platoon strong new unit charged with protecting the Sultan's person. Sultan Ghalib II had designed their uniforms based on what was locally available. A number of SLR rifles were made available and Col. Phil Hillman

(Military Assistant to Resident Adviser) drilled and trained them with the new weapon.

RIYAN GUARDS

HARAS AL RIYAN

AFRICAN COMPANY

During the 1940s former slaves and some Somalis were recruited for an airfield protection company known as the 'African Company'. This was tasked with guarding RAF Riyan, located a few miles outside of Mukalla. To ensure that the company received the necessary military training a King's African Rifles sergeant major was sent to Riyan. The unit, belonging to the Mukalla Regular Army, was commanded by an Indian Army officer. In about 1948 the unit was disbanded, and a new force formed.

RIYAN GUARDS

The new company undertook the same role, but now consisted of former gendarmerie Yafa'is living in the nearby Boweish village east of Riyan and Seiban tribesmen from the hills to the north. They are reported to have worn sky blue *pagri* and below-the-knee-length khaki shirts. The commander was a Yafa'i *Mulazim* or lieutenant, who had retired from the Mukalla Regular Army. In about 1960 he was replaced by a Deyyini tribesman from the Hadhrami Bedouin Legion, who had served in the Nizam of Hyderabad's Bodyguard for 17 years before joining the HBL Upon his arrival the Riyan Guards came under HBL influence and changed from MRA-style uniform to that of the HBL

ROYAL AIR FORCE

The Royal Air Force and its predecessor the Royal Flying Corps became involved with Aden in 1916. It was during that year when the seaplane carrier HMS *Raven II*, which carried six aircraft, was transferred from Port Said, Egypt, to Aden. The ship's aircraft carried out a series of raids on Turkish positions. This demonstration of air power was used both to damage the Turkish war machine and to influence the local Arab population. The latter became a function that was to prove very successful in controlling Aden Protectorate during the 1930s. 114 Squadron, RFC, was formed at Lahore, India, in September 1917 from a nucleus provided by No. 31 Squadron. A Flight of 114 Squadron (RAF) was stationed in Aden by September 1918. On 4 April 1928 the Air Ministry assumed responsibility for the defence of Aden from the War Office. This included control of the Aden Protectorate Levies.

In 1928 there were troubles in the Protectorate emanating from Yemen. The previous year Yemen forces were only 40 miles from Aden. Air action was authorised by HM Government and the headquarters and garrisons of the military forces of Yemen were bombed. Eventually the Iman's forces evacuated Dhala, which had been occupied and returned to Yemen. No. 8 Squadron RAF achieved this success in two months. Over the following years the RAF were involved in a number of actions against both incursions of armed tribesmen into Protectorate territory and inter-tribal disturbances. In many cases the threat of air action alone was sufficient to bring about a settlement. Another RAF task was to safeguard Aden against seaborne attack during wartime, and to control and protect the southern approaches to the Red Sea. Aden was supplemented by several more RAF squadrons during the Second World War, including a Flight of Free French Marylands. On 12 June 1940 operations commenced against Italian aerodromes in Abyssinia and Eritrea. The Blenheims, Vincents and Gladiators of the command flew reconnaissance, bombing and anti-submarine sweeps. On 19 June 1940 an Italian submarine was attacked by a small naval vessel and a Vincent of No. 8 Squadron and surrendered intact. The primary mission of the Aden squadrons was to support the campaigns in Abyssinia. In October 1943 they helped quell rebel elements in Ethiopia. Later in the war a plane from No. 8 Squadron assisted in attacking a German U-boat, which was beached and scuttled.

A completely different task arose in 1944 when a famine flight was established to carry food daily to Quatan in the Hadhramaut. This was repeated in early 1949 when famine struck again. Transport aircraft from the Middle East Air Force were sent to RAF Riyan, in Qu'aiti State in the Hadhramaut. From there they carried out an airlift of grain to a secluded valley in the Hadhramaut as thousands of people faced starvation. Between 4 February and 2 March 1949, RAF Dakotas dropped 750 tons of grain, thus averting disaster.

Following the war, the RAF in Aden became almost devoid of operational units. Only 621 (GR) Squadron, which consisted of Wellingtons, remained at RAF Khormaksar for surveillance of the Red Sea, Gulf of Aden and the Arabian Sea.

Table 12: RAF units were based in South Arabia

Hedjuff Aden	Marine Craft Unit 206 216 and 220 Air/Sea Rescue Units
Jhadir	Armoured Car Section
Khormaksar	RAF Station comprising: 621 (GR) Squadron (Wellingtons) HQ BF Aden Communication Flight 1566 Meteorological Flight 114 Squadron (Bostons)
Riyan	RAF Station
Sheikh Othman	Aden Protectorate Levies
Socotra	RAF Socotra
Steamer Point	RAF Station comprising: Equipment and Supply Section 50 Embarkation Unit 7 RAF Hospital 11 RAF Postal HQ 3 Base Personnel Office 6 Works Area 5721 Mechanical and Electrical Flight Aircraft Safety Centre, Southern Arabia Area Control, Aden 21 Rifle Squadron
Wadi Road	Aden Telecommunications Centre (Aden)

In 1948, the Governor requested the deployment of 20 Wing, RAF Regiment, to act in an internal security and anti-riot role within the colony. The unit was also tasked with reinforcing Somaliland in the event of an emergency. The Wing comprised 58 and 66 Rifle Squadrons with a total strength of about 300 officers and airmen. In addition, a detachment of about 30 was sent to Mweiga, Kenya, as airstrip protection.

By 1952 the following units were under the control of HQ British Forces in Aden and the Protectorates:

Belvedere HC.1 of 26 Squadron RAF up-country Aden on makeshift landing pad, 1962. (Joint Public Relations Unit Aden)

Table 13: RAF Squadrons in Aden, 1956

Aden Communications	8 Valettas and Pembrokes, 2 Sycamore Helicopters
8 Squadron	16 Venoms
78 Squadron	6 Twin Pioneers
1426 Flight	4 Lincolns
20 Wing RAF Regiment	58 and 66 Field Squadrons

RAF Khormaksar
RAF Steamer Point
RAF Riyan
8 (Light Bomber) Squadron
HQ 20 Wing RAF Regiment
HQ Aden Protectorate Levies
HQ 51 Coast Regiment
HQ Troop, 65 Wing, Royal Signals

Table 14: Operational units permanently located at RAF Khormaksar, 1 January 1964

8 Squadron	12 Hunter FGA.9
43 Squadron	12 Hunter FGA.9
208 Squadron	12 Hunter FGA.9
26 Squadron	7 Belvedere HC.1
37 Squadron	4 Shackleton MR.2
78 Squadron	8 Twin Pioneer CCI (later Wessex helicopters)
84 Squadron	6 Beverley C.1
105 Squadron	10 Argosy C.1
233 Squadron	6 Valetta C.1
1417 Flight	4 Hunter FR.10
SAR Flight	3 Sycamore HR.14

RAF Hospital Aden (opened prior to the Second World War)
APL Hospital
7 Anti-Malarial Unit
RAF Communication Centre

HQ British Forces Aden also had functional control of the following units:

114 Maintenance Unit
131 Maintenance Unit
1152 Marine Craft Unit
50 RAF Movements Unit
Aden Supply Depot
5004 (Airfield Construction) Squadron from 1959 to 1966

Over the years the composition of the RAF units in Aden altered as dictated by the circumstances. The number and strength of the squadrons reflect the seriousness of the security situation at any given time. Upon the British departure from Aden the squadrons either transferred to other RAF stations in the Gulf or were disbanded.

8 SQUADRON ROYAL AIR FORCE ADEN

Although many RAF squadrons deployed to Aden over the years, 8 Squadron spent more time there than any others and deserves to be recorded here. Responding to unrest in the hinterland in February 1927, 8 Squadron, RAF, was deployed to RAF Khormaksar where it continued in the air policing role it had been involved with when in Iraq. The squadron replaced its de Havilland DH.9As with new Fairey IIIF light bombers from January 1928 and flew operations against Zaidi tribesmen in February 1928 and against the Subaihi tribe in the west who revolted and refused to pay tax. Operations in 1929 against the Subaihi involved destroying crops with incendiary bombs and bombing villages after giving

RAF GMC Otter Armoured cars of 4001 Flight about to patrol Dhala Road, post-Second World War. Note the RAF roundel on the back of the vehicle. (Sean Brady)

Side view of RAF GMC Otter Armoured car of 4001 Flight in Aden. (Sean Brady)

advanced warning so they could be evacuated. The Subaihi eventually sued for peace, and paid fines. Other tasks, included survey flights, were carried out as well as casualty evacuation and carrying mail. Vickers Vincent's were introduced in 1935 and were a general purpose aircraft based on the Vickers Vildebeest biplane torpedo bomber. These in turn were replaced by Bristol Blenheim bombers in 1939, but a flight of Vincent's was retained for operations over the rough interior.

Table 15: RAF Squadrons and Flights that were based in Aden

Unit	Date	Comment/Aircraft
Flight, 114 Squadron	1918–1920	BE.2 aircraft
8 Squadron	1927–1945 1946–1967	1945–1945 in India. (See history for list of aircraft types flown by the squadron)
12 Squadron	1935–1936	Hawker Hart
41 Squadron	1935–1936	Hawker Demon. To Sheikh Othman 1936
94 Squadron	1939–1941	Gloster Gladiator I & II
11 Squadron	1940–1941	Bristol Blenheim
39 Squadron	1940	Bristol Blenheim
203 Squadron	1940–1941	Bristol Blenheim IV
459 Squadron RAAF	1942–1944	Aden and Socotra Island. Lockheed Hudson III. Detached from LG227 & LG143
621 Squadron	1943–1945	Vickers Wellington XIII
259 Squadron	1943–1945	Consolidated Catalina IB detached from Dar es Salaam
265 Squadron	1943–1945	Consolidated Catalina IB detached from Dar es Salaam
244 Squadron	1944–1945	Vickers Wellington. Detached from Masirah

Unit	Date	Comment/Aircraft
73 Squadron	1956–1957	Detached During Suez Crisis. De Havilland Venom FB.1
78 Squadron	1956–1967	Scottish Aviation Pioneer CC1
37 Squadron	1957–1967	Avro Shackleton MR.2
84 Squadron	1960–1967	Vickers Valetta, Bristol Sycamore, Percival Pembroke, Blackburn Beverley, HS Andover
233 Squadron	1960–1964	Vickers Valetta C.1
208 Squadron	1961–1964	Hawker Hunter FGA.9 Detached from RAF Akrotiri
105 Squadron	1962–1967	Armstrong Whitworth Argosy C.1
26 Squadron	1963–1965	Bristol Belvedere HC.1
43 Squadron	1963–1967	Hawker Hunter FGA.9
21 Squadron	1965–1967	Douglas Dakota, HS Andover
1417 Flight	1956–1960	Arabian Reconnaissance Flight. Gloster Meteor FR.9
1426 Flight	1956–1956	Photographic Reconnaissance. Avro Lincoln
1417 Flight	1963–1967	Hawker Hunter FR.10/T.7 Fighter Reconnaissance
D Flight, 8 Squadron RAF	1928–1929	Armoured cars Khormaksar
RAF Armoured Car Section	1929–1947	Khormaksar. To 4001 Armoured Car Flight 1947 Royal Air Force Regiment
5004 Airfield Construction Squadron RAF	1959–1964	Khormaksar

Italy declared war on Britain and France on 10 June 1940 and 8 Squadron flew its first combat mission on 12 June when nine Blenheim's flew over the Red Sea to Italian-occupied Eritrea and bombed the airfield at Assab. On 5 August 1940 Italy invaded British Somaliland, and 8 Squadron's Blenheim's were used to attack advancing Italian troop columns. The Italians heavily outnumbered the British and Commonwealth defences, and consequently the port of Berbera was occupied by the Italians on 19 August. From December 1943 until May 1945 Vickers Wellingtons were flown by the squadron. The squadron reformed in May at Jessore, India as 200 Squadron and flew Consolidated Liberator V but disbanded on 15 November 1945 and reformed at RAF Khormaksar Aden on 1 September 1946 by renumbering No. 114 Squadron. Mosquito FB.6 fighter bomber aircraft were their new aircraft, which were later replaced by Hawker Tempest, Bristol Brigand and in 1953 de Havilland Vampire FB.9 jets replaced the previous piston engine aircraft. The Vampires gave way to de Havilland Venom FB.1s and FB.4s and finally Hawker Hunter FGA.9 and T.7 and FR.10s in 1960 where they remained until leaving Aden in 1967. Because of the squadron's long association with the Middle East it seemed appropriate to adopt the Arabian Khunjah as the unit's emblem.

ROYAL AIR FORCE REGIMENT IN ADEN

The Royal Air Force Regiment is a part of the Royal Air Force, and is a highly professional unit of RAF soldiers who are specialised in the numerous tasks for the defence of airfields. When in Aden the units carried out soldiering tasks with the APL which included training, commanding units and manning armoured cars. The APL was under RAF command until 1957 when the Army took responsibility for the Levies. After 1957 the squadrons of the regiment had a mainly defensive role responsible for the complex task of airfield protection, although 16 Squadron, RAF Regiment did provide a mortar detachment in the Radfan ca 1964.

Table 16: RAF Regiment in Aden

4001 Armoured Car Flight, Royal Air Force Regiment	1947–1950	moved to Amman, Jordan
20 Wing, RAF Regiment	1948	disbanded at Khormaksar 1957
58 Rifle Squadron, RAF Regiment	1948	disbanded at Khormaksar 1957
66 Rifle Squadron, RAF Regiment	1948	disbanded at Khormaksar 1957
62 Squadron, RAF Regiment	1955	1956
48 Field Squadron, RAF Regiment	1962	1963
16 Squadron, RAF Regiment	1964	1965 Mortar Detachment Radfan
27 Squadron, RAF Regiment	1965	1965
34 Squadron, RAF Regiment	1965	1965
2 Squadron, RAF Regiment	1965	1966
37 Squadron, RAF Regiment	1966	1966
66 Squadron, RAF Regiment	1966	1967
48 Squadron, RAF Regiment	1966	1967
51 Squadron, RAF Regiment	1967	1967
2 Squadron, RAF Regiment	1965	1966
2 Squadron, RAF Regiment	1967	1967
10 Armoured Car Squadron, APL	1955	1957 RAF Regiment Crew

When 20 Wing, RAF Regiment arrived in Aden in 1948 it consisted of a Wing Headquarters and 58 and 66 Rifle Squadrons. Later Rifle Squadrons converted formally by re-role training to become Field Squadrons. Rifle Squadrons were infantry units of three flights and a 3-inch mortar Flight. Field Squadrons were mobile recce units with Land Rovers and comprised of four flights and were armed with more light machine guns.

RAF SIGNAL UNITS

19 Signals Unit
22 Tactical Signals Unit
123 Signals Unit
198 Signals Unit
303 Signals Unit
402 Signals Unit

A member of the RAF Regiment. Of interest is the locally made cross jambia beret badge, mid 1950s. (Brian Bailey)

RAF Saltpans Transmitter
RAF Khormaksar
Station motto: *Into the Remote Places*

Khormaksar airfield opened in 1917 and had a major upgraded in 1945. Not only was the airfield the main Royal Air Force Station in Aden and the Protectorates in the 1960s but it was also the busiest RAF Station in the world as it doubled up as an international civil airport. The Army Air Corps used the airfield too with their Austers, Beavers and Scouts as well as aircraft from visiting Royal Navy warships. There were 15 charter companies and airlines plus private operators that used the facilities including Aden Airways DC3s, East African Airways Comets, Air India Boeing 707s and Vickers VC10s. The station was mainly concerned with maintaining scheduled air services within the command and with supplying ground forces stationed up-country at bases which could not be reached by other means of transport – to which end the station maintained a number of air strips in the Protectorates and in Muscat and Oman. The RAF Station closed on 29 November 1967 when the Peoples Republic of South Yemen gained independence.

RAF Khormaksar in the mid-1960s consisted of the following units:

TACTICAL/STRIKE WING

Hunter and Belvedere units were based at Khormaksar until December 1964 when the Shackleton squadron arrived. Consequently, the structure was changed and split into Strike Wing, with Belvederes moving to Transport Wing.

HELICOPTER FLIGHT

The Sycamore HR.14 helicopters' role was search and rescue, and to take casualties to Aden for hospital treatment. Helicopters were in Khormaksar from late 1955 and became a separate Flight in 1958. At times the helicopters were required to support operations in Trucial Oman in 1959, Bahrain in 1960 and on one occasion to give a display at the Royal Agricultural Show in Nairobi. Sycamores were replaced by Whirlwind HAR.10s in 1964.

AIR TRAFFIC CONTROL SQUADRON

Responsible for the safety of all aircraft, both civil and military, in the air and on the ground. Squadron tasks included control of aircraft in the air to prevent collisions and supplying information to all aircraft within its area. In addition to the airfield itself, Air Traffic Control supervised a Control Zone that extended to a 40-mile circumference of the airfield.

MARINE CRAFT UNIT

Formed in about 1934, the MCU was based first at Obstruction Pier, Aden, then Maalla and finally back to Obstruction Pier. MCU had a 24-hour search and rescue commitment. Their main work was taking supplies to route stations as far as Bahrain using 200 ton 'Z'-craft. 206, 214, 215, 216 and 220 Air Sea Rescue Units were disestablished and formed in their place was one Marine Craft Unit (1152 MCU) in Aden with small detachments operating from Masirah, Salalah and Mukalla. 1152 Marine Craft Unit 1952–1967 was employed in Maritime rescue.

DESERT RESCUE

The search and rescue units at Khormaksar included a small group of volunteers for Mountain and Desert Rescue operations. Formed in 1963, they were the youngest of the RAF's mountain rescue units.

TRANSPORT WING

Transport Wing included three squadrons of transport aircraft and the Air Movements Section. The Officer Commanding Transport Wing's responsibilities included the up-country airstrips in the Aden Protectorate and the route airfields along the South Arabian Coast.

MIDDLE EAST AIR FORCE COMMUNICATIONS FLIGHT

Many RAF stations operated a Communications Flight and that at Khormaksar, in the early 1960s, had an allocation of two Canberra B.2s painted in an all-over white livery, a Hastings C.4 and Valetta C.2, and a Dakota C.4 maintained by civilian DC-3 technicians from Aden Airways, and was normally parked and operated from the civil airport. The Canberras were scrapped behind the SAR Flight hangar in early 1964. In the mid-sixties, and renamed Middle East Communications Squadron, the Unit was allocated a second Dakota C.4 and an Andover C.1.

FIRE SECTION

Airfield Fire Station Section was on watch 24 hours a day.

AIR MOVEMENTS SECTION

This section handled all the passengers and freight carried by the Khormaksar-based squadrons and the RAF aircraft passing through.

TECHNICAL WING

Aircraft maintenance was the task of the Technical Wing including the Helicopter Flight, Marine Craft, Motor Transport, Engines, Airframes, Electrical Instruments, radio, ground radio, armament and the Command Photographic Section. The Technical Wing had two sections, one dealing with regular servicing of aircraft and 131 Maintenance Unit, which specialised in heavy repair work.

131 MAINTENANCE UNIT

131 MU was established at Khormaksar at the end of 1958 to provide heavy repair facilities for all technical equipment in the Command. It comprised three flights, handling repair and salvage of aircraft, repair of motor transport and general engineering.

Belvedere HC.1 OF 26 Squadron RAF transporting a heavy load, 1962. (Joint Public Relations Unit Aden)

A fourth section, the Electronic Repair Squadron, was later established to maintain radio and radar equipment.

REORGANISATION

A major reorganisation of RAF Khormaksar Station occurred on 14 December 1964. Station OC Operations Wing and OC Technical Wing were placed in a special position as staff officers to the Station Commander for operational matters and technical matters respectively. Operations Wing came under the command of a Wing Commander, general duties, responsible for control of the Station Operations Centre and the flying support units. In addition, he was responsible to the Station Commander for the tasking of all aircraft, advising him on all matters affecting the fulfilment of the station's operational task as directed by Headquarters Middle East Command.

FLYING WINGS

The two flying Wings were increased to three Wings as follows:
Strike Wing
Strike Wing was formed from Tactical Wing on 14 December 1964 and remained under the command of the then current OC Tactical Wing. It then consisted of 8 and 43 Squadrons (Hunter FGA.9), No. 1417 Flight (Hunter FR.10), No. 37 Squadron (Shackleton MR.2), and Strike Wing Servicing Squadron.
Medium Range Transport (MRT) Wing
MRT Wing was placed under the command of the current OC 105 Squadron (Argosies), becoming OC MRT Wing and 105 Squadron. The Wing comprised 105 Squadron (Argosies), 84 Squadron (Beverleys) and MRT Servicing Squadron.
Short Range Transport (SRT) Wing
SRT Wing remained under the command of the current OC Transport Wing and consisted of No. 26 Squadron (Belvederes), No. 78 Squadron (Twin Pioneers), Middle East Communications Squadron, Search and Rescue Flight and SRT Servicing Squadron.

RAF STEAMER POINT

Steamer Point was where the original garrison had been established and where Headquarters, Middle East (Aden) Command was situated. RAF Steamer Point provided the administrative services for most units in the base area. The Commanding Officer was responsible for the RAF Aden Communications Centre, 114 Maintenance Unit, the Aden Supply Depot, 50 Movement Unit, the HQ Provost and Security Services, staff at Command HQ, the RAF Hospital, the Aden Protectorate Levies Hospital, 7 Anti-Malarial Unit and 222 Signal Squadron Royal Signals, which maned the telephone exchange and maintained landlines up-country.

COMMUNICATIONS CENTRE

Serving the unified HQ of Middle East (Aden) Command, the RAF Communications Centre provided the communications for all three Services – Contact with the rest of the world was by high-speed radio teleprinter networks linking Aden with all Commonwealth and NATO military forces. Morse radio circuits to some destinations still existed at that time.

114 MU

114 Maintenance Unit was a RAF Equipment Depot, which supplied equipment of all kinds to the RAF and, to a limited extent, to Army and Navy units in the Command. The unit had blacksmiths, sheet metalworkers, carpenters and a fabric shop to make items for both the military and the airman's families.

RAF HOSPITAL

The RAF Hospital was situated on the hills overlooking Steamer Point. Originally it had been an Indian Army Medical Service Hospital before the RAF took over in the 1920s. The facility provided British Forces and families with 180 beds, and also merchant seamen of all nationalities. Staffing of the hospital was by RAF Medical Service doctors and orderlies, Princess Mary's Royal Air Force Nursing Service sisters and WRAF orderlies.

SUPPLY DEPOT

The RAF Aden Supply Depot provided food for all the RAF and Army units including the APL within in the Colony and Protectorate, and visiting Royal Navy ships. The Supply Depot was taken over by the RAF from the Royal Indian Army Corps in 1946.

50 MOVEMENT UNIT

This unit was responsible for baggage of the RAF servicemen and their families when moving in or out of Aden.

WRAF

About 50 Women's Royal Airforce personnel were stationed in Aden. Their trades included clerks, typists, shorthand typists, telephonists and telegraphists working at HQ MEC, RAF Steamer Point and the Communications Centre. Store-women were at 114 Maintenance Unit, nursing orderlies at the hospital. The WRAF also provided a dental hygienist and a dental surgery attendant and a PT instructor.

RAF RIYAN

The coastal airfield of RAF Riyan was located near the city of Mukalla in the Qu'aiti State in the Eastern Aden Protectorate and was 273 miles north-east along the coast from Aden. The sandy airstrip was built in 1945. As a route station, Riyan was primarily concerned with the refuelling of RAF aircraft that operated along the South Arabian route, although much of the traffic handled was civilian. Aden Airways DC-3 aircraft flew in and out almost every day, maintaining the civilian airline link between Aden and the Eastern Aden Protectorate, particularly the Wadi Hadhramaut region. Because of the volume of civilian schedule traffic, Riyan was a very busy airfield for its size. Riyan was run by a staff of two officers and 30 airmen.

ROYAL NAVY

Early naval activity in the Aden area was conducted by the Bombay Marine, but the Royal Navy played an increasingly important role during the nineteenth century when the area formed part of the East Indies Station. In 1830 the Bombay Marine became the Indian Navy and following the Indian Mutiny was transferred to the crown in 1858. Five years later it was reduced to non-combatant status. From 1877 onwards it gradually regained its role as a fighting service. For many years there was only a very small naval presence in Aden as it was regarded as little more than an offshoot of the Commander-in-Chief (C-in-C) East Indies Headquarters at Ceylon.

Although Aden possessed a Royal Navy wireless telegraphy station at Khormaksar, it was not until 22 January 1935 that a named naval base, HMS *Norfolk III*, was established. On 1 April 1940 the

Commando Carrier R07 HMS *Albion* in Aden Harbour 1962. (Joint Public Relations Unit Aden)

from HMS *Centaur* ferried troops and supplies to the front line, and Sea Vixens flew reconnaissance, photographic and strike sorties against the rebel tribesmen. Royal Naval Fleet Air Arm and Royal Marine forces continued to be deployed as required during the period of the Emergency. The Fleet Air Arm had on occasion the following Naval Air Squadrons in Aden including 815 and 826 Naval Air Squadrons and 848 Naval Air Commando Squadron. From March 1965 until the withdrawal in 1967 a coastal minesweeper was permanently deployed at Aden in the anti-dissident role.

The withdrawal from Aden in November 1967 marked the end of the Middle East Command and the British civil and military presence in Aden and the Protectorate. The High Commissioner and the last British forces finally departed on 29 November. The final phases of the naval withdrawal from Aden were conducted by the Flag Officer Second in Command Far East Fleet at sea, in command of Task Force 318, which provided seaborne cover to the entire operation. TF 318 included two aircraft carriers, two commando carriers, two assault ships and a guided missile destroyer, plus many lesser warships. Below is a list of the principal ships that took part in the evacuation.

45 COMMANDO ROYAL MARINES

Between 1960 and 1967, 45 Commando was based in Aden and undertook 10 operational tours in the Radfan during the Aden Emergency. The last elements of the Commando left Aden on 29 November 1967.

42 COMMANDO ROYAL MARINES

42 Commando, located on HMS *Albion*, a former aircraft carrier converted to the Commando Carrier role, visited Aden in 1962. The vessel took part in the evacuation of the last units of the British armed forces in October and November 1967.

ROYAL SIGNALS

In 1927, Royal Signals took over the Aden Signal Section from the Indian Signal Corps. Staff at the Royal Signals Museum indicate men were still being posted to the Aden Signal Section as late as 1930, but there is no further mention of this unit in the Corps history of Royal Signals or Indian Signals. On 1 February 1949, the Aden Command Signal Troop was redesignated Aden Air Formation Signal Troop, and in September 1949 it became 65 Wing Troop, a distant part of 4 Air Formation Signal Regiment, which was based in Egypt. Records show that HQ Troop 65 Wing Royal Signals was still in Aden in 1951, and it may have remained there until 1958–1959.

base was renamed HMS *Sheba* and located at Tawahi. A converted trawler, HMT *Moonstone*, captured the Italian Submarine *Galileo Galilei* off Aden on 19 June 1940. HMT *Moonstone* was part of the 4th Anti-Submarine Group based at Malta and was later transferred to Alexandria to patrol off Aden. While on patrol she located an Italian submarine and on her second run of depth charges forced the submarine to surface. HMT *Moonstone* then assaulted the submarine head on with gunfire forcing the submarine crew to surrender. Shortly after the destroyer HMS *Kandahar* arrived to give assistance with prisoners and towing the submarine. HMT *Moonstone* entered Aden followed by its prize and HMS *Kandahar*. Eventually the Italian submarine was taken into Royal Naval service. On 11 June 1941 an expedition was mounted from Aden to capture the Italian-held port of Assab, in Eritrea on the Red Sea, and a contraband control organisation was established. A few enemy submarines were sighted during the war, and early in 1943 a defensive minefield was laid in the Straits of Bab-el-Mandeb. As the war progressed the role of HMS *Sheba* expanded considerably. Its outstations included Port Sudan and Kilindini, the port of Mombasa in Kenya.

From 1945 until 1961, when the unified Middle East Command was instituted, HMS *Sheba*'s importance diminished. This was the first unified, or joint service command introduced post-war, and the C-in-C Middle East and his staff was based at Aden. The navy's Arabian Seas and Persian Gulf Station was abolished and the Flag Officer Arabian Seas and Persian Gulf became the Flag Officer, Middle East (FOME), responsible to the C-in-C Middle East. FOME transferred his flag from HMS *Jufair* at Bahrain to HMS *Sheba* in 1962. During the post-war period the Royal Navy was involved in a number of anti-dissident operations in Aden and the Protectorate, principally deploying fixed and rotary wing aircraft of the Fleet Air Arm and providing support from seaward to land operations. Among these were operations against the tribesmen of the Radfan in 1964, in which 45 Commando Royal Marines participated as an infantry battalion. Helicopters

ADEN AIR FORMATION SIGNAL TROOP

Created from Aden Command Signal Troop in 1949.

65 WING TROOP, 4 AIR FORMATION SIGNAL REGIMENT

The Troop was formed from the Aden Air Formation Signal Troop in 1949.

403 WIRELESS DETACHMENT ADEN

The detachment was sent from 2 Wireless Regiment Cyprus in January 1957. It consisted of two Intelligence Corps personnel, and about eight radio operators, a driver, a radio technician and a detachment officer. The role of the unit was to eves-drop on wireless transmissions within the Yemen.

HQ BRITISH FORCES ARABIAN PENINSULA (INDEPENDENT) SIGNAL SQUADRON

HQ British Forces Arabian Peninsula (Independent) Signal Squadron was raised in 1958 and lasted until 1959/1960.

254 SIGNAL SQUADRON (ADEN)

HQ British Forces Arabian Peninsula (Independent) Signal Squadron was disbanded in 1959/1960 and 254 Signal Squadron (Aden) was raised. It in turn disbanded in 1965 when its duties were absorbed into 15 Signal Regiment. (Note: The squadron was reformed in 1971 at Cyprus).

222 (AIR FORMATION) SIGNAL SQUADRON

The squadron may have had links to HQ Troop 65 Wing Royal Signals. With the disbandment of HQ British Forces Arabian Peninsula (Independent) Signal Squadron in Aden in 1959/1960, 222 Signal Squadron was raised with the task of coordinating ground/air operations in Arabia and East Africa. Relocation to Sharjah took place in June 1967 but leaving K Troop with 15 Signal Regiment.

603 SIGNAL TROOP

The Troop was originally formed within British Forces Arabian Peninsula Signal Squadron as Signal Troop Kenya in 1959. The Troop was later absorbed into 15 Signal Regiment for use as Forward Air Control Detachments.

643 (COMMS SECURITY) SIGNAL TROOP

Raised in Aden in 1964 as Communications Security Troop where it focused on eavesdropping on Yemen. The unit was absorbed into 15 Signal Regiment in 1965.

15 SIGNAL REGIMENT

With the increasing need for communications in Aden, 15 Signal Regiment was raised on 22 January 1965. This regiment absorbed 254 and 255 (Bahrain) Signal Squadrons, 603 Signal Troop and 643 (Comms Security) Signal Troop.

The regiment consisted of:

1 Squadron COMCEN and Cipher
2 Squadron Radio
3 Squadron (located in Bahrain)

The Troops included:

D Troop, Steamer Point
E Troop, Isthmus

F Troop, Falaise Camp, Little Aden
K Troop, Airport
J Troop, Joint HQ
L Troop, Aden Brigade
TM Troop, System Control

The role of the regiment was to provide line and radio communications to the Middle East. It operated against a background of terrorist attacks and civil unrest until disbanded in October 1967. A rearguard squadron remained for a few more weeks. The regiment was located at Singapore Lines, Khormaksar, and provided communications for Aden Brigade and had a Troop (F) at Little Aden. A communication centre detachment was located at the FRA camp in Seedaseer Lines, and a self-contained radio/cipher detachment was provided for the Resident Adviser in Mukalla. The regiment made available technical personnel, linemen or operators anywhere within South Arabia when required and sometimes to Africa. Its sign was an Egyptian cat with a Roman XV. This reflected the regiment's origin, as it was first raised in Egypt in 1940.

210 SIGNAL SQUADRON

The squadron was sent to Aden in 1964 as part of 24 Infantry Brigade from East Africa and remained in Aden until August 1967.

213 SIGNAL SQUADRON

As part of 39 Infantry Brigade (Air Portable) the squadron saw service in Aden during 1964.

SCHOOL FOR THE IMPROVEMENT OF ARMY UNITS

MADRASAT TAHSEEN AL-WAHDAAT

The School for the Improvement of Army Units was a military academy situated in Mukalla. The institution was formed by Harold Ingrams and paid for by HM Government. Various outdoor facilities were used for the field activities. Some of the lecturing premises were in the residency compound in the old fort (Husn al-Shaybah). The accommodation facilities were on top of the Mukalla gateway, referred to by the British as Marble Arch. The commandant of the Academy, Omar Ba Sa'id held the rank of

The Mukalla Military Academy's last intake receiving their prizes at their HQ on top of the Mukalla Gateway in November 1966. H.H. Sultan Ghalib al Qu'aiti presenting NCO Ali Ahmed Bahabri of the MRA with a prize. In the background on the left: Captain Salim 'Abdullah al Fardi (ADC to the Sultan) and to his right is Major Faraj 'Abdul Habeeb al- Jahwari (Deputy Commandant of the MRA). (Sultan Ghalib)

The last intake to graduate from the School for the Improvement of Army Units, which was the local military academy. Left to right: a lecturer, Academy Commandant Major 'Omar Ba'l Haj, Acting Wazir 'Abdul-Rahman Bazargan, Amir 'Omar al Qu'aiti, Sultan Ghalib al Qu'aiti, Jim Ellis OBE (Resident Adviser and British Agent), Lt. Col. Hillman (Military Assistant to the Resident Adviser) and an instructor. British Residency courtyard November 1966. (Sultan Ghalib)

The Mukalla Military Academy's last intake receiving their prizes at their HQ on top of the Mukalla Gateway in November 1966. H.H. Sultan Ghalib al Qu'aiti presenting NCO Ali Ahmed Bahabri of the MRA with a prize. In the background on the left: Captain Salim 'Abdullah al Fardi (ADC to the Sultan) and to his right is Major Faraj 'Abdul Habeeb al- Jahwari (Deputy Commandant of the MRA). (Sultan Ghalib)

major. Various instructors were used for the different subjects for lecturing purposes.

All NCOs with officer potential were made to attend the school before promotion, as were all Qu'aiti *Qa'ims* (District Commissioners). Several Amirs from the neighbouring States were graduates, as was Sultan Ghalib's brother Omar. The curriculum, apart from military training, included all subjects of administrative relevance such as law, history, geography and writing reports. It was one of the most useful institutions to be supported by HM Government. It ceased to exist by mid-1967.

SOUTH ARABIAN ARMY

JAISH AL JANOB

On 1 June 1967 the South Arabian Army was formed from the FRA and FNG. With the impending departure of Britain from South Arabia it was deemed necessary to consolidate and unify the disparate forces within the country. It was argued that Arabisation was a high priority and rationalisation of the various forces was essential to a successful defence force. It was intended that the Hadhrami Bedouin Legion would also be included when the Eastern Aden Protectorate States joined the Federation. The reality

of the merger was that very little change took place, other than the FRA exchanging its headdress badge and shoulder title for SAA insignia. The FNG continued to wear its old badges and beret for some time after amalgamation.

In *Last Post Aden 1964–67*, Julian Paget states that on 7 November 1967 the SAA 'abandoned their former loyalties to the Federation; they changed their title to the Arab Armed Forces in Occupied South Yemen'. British forces rapidly left and by the end of November 1967 all had vacated the country, the former SAA becoming the Army of the People's Democratic Republic of Yemen.

UNIFORM

The badge of the SAA was similar to the FRA but with a green scroll and a larger star and crescent. An anodized green shoulder title was issued. The uniform of the SAA was the same as the FRA.

Mine-proofed vehicle locally manufactured/modified by the SAA EME workshops. Note the mine-proofed cab. (Peter Herrett)

SAA soldier of HQ Squadron with captured Kalashnikov and spare magazine holder, Seedaseer Lines, Aden 1967. (Tony Ford)

SAA HQ Squadron driver with a green and white lanyard armed with Sterling SMG stands in front of a Staff Land Rover at Seedaseer Lines, Aden 1967. The TAC sign is HQ Squadron green over white diagonally. (Tony Ford)

Staff Sergeant Tony Ford, Chief Clerk G Branch, with Corporal Clerk at Seedaseer Lines, Aden 1967. (Tony Ford)

SOUTH ARABIAN POLICE

AL SHURTAH AL ARABI'A AL JUNUBIYA

Concurrent with the formation of the South Arabian Army on 1 June 1967, the South Arabian Police was formed from the Aden Police and the units of the Federal National Guard 2 (FNG2). Thus, it was envisaged that, in one stroke, all of the armed constabularies and police forces of the federation would become a single force. However, before this could happen the whole system began to unravel due to the civil war, and many of the old FNG2 units ceased to exist. Jonathan Walker in his book Aden

Insurgency states that the Aden Armed Police were controlled not by the Federal Government but by the British High Commission. Their insignia was identical to the Civil Police. No dress or insignia changes took place with the formation of the SAP. After the departure of the British from Aden and pending the design and manufacture of a new one, the cap badge was modified by the simple expedient of cutting off the crown.

SPECIAL GUARD

Special Guard was an irregular force paid for by the Amir of Dhala out of funds provided by Her Majesty's Government. The Guard, supposedly loyal to the Amir, was on ad hoc duties such as guarding the airfield against minelaying. This force was active circa 1965–1967. Special Guard was also present in Audhali and Beihan. There was no discipline or formal uniform.

SULTAN AWADH BIN OMER'S ARAB REGIMENT

JAMAIYYAT-E-'UROOB-E-SHAMSHIR UL MULK BAHADUR

The Nizam of Hyderabad's forces in India had a component of troops maintained and commanded by the nobility. One of these battalions was commanded by Sultan Awadh bin Omer's father. 'Jamadar' Omer bin Awadh had been charged with maintaining a force of 2,500 Arab soldiers in Hyderabad, India, from the Hadhramaut and Yafa (the tribe from which he hailed). For this he was awarded vast tracts of revenue bearing territory. Command of his battalion was later divided between an elder son, Saleh bin Omer and his brother Sultan Awadh bin Omer. The former was awarded charge of two-thirds of his father's force, whereas the latter received the remaining third, the strength of which was increased later to nearly 1,100 Arab soldiers. The strength of this force was to be divided again after him between his son Sultan Omer bin Awadh and grandson Sultan Saleh bin Ghalib, with each receiving a half. The battalion included a component of cavalry and artillery. However, until the signing of the Advisory Treaty of 1936 with the British by the Qu'aiti Sultan, and the appointment of a Resident Adviser and British Agent in Mukalla, the Qu'aiti family tended to treat their assets, whether in Arabia or India, as one and the same and would refer to them officially as 'Amlaak al-Qatah' (the possessions of the Qu'aiti family). Since the revenue from the Hadhramaut was insufficient for policing and administering the territory, the income from the assets in India was used to subsidise it to the tune of 40 percent and more. Any military activity or otherwise involving heavy financing (such as the expedition to annex Hajar and its subsequent purchase from the tribes) was also covered by the sale of assets in India. Officers and men of this force in Hyderabad were also discreetly used in operations in the Hadhramaut from time to time after being officially dismissed. This was in order to satisfy British requirement that men of the Nizam of Hyderabad's forces should not be used in operations beyond India without their approval. The smart ceremonial Indian uniforms were introduced into the Hadhramaut from Hyderabad. At the Delhi Durbar of 1911 the Sultan of Shehr and Mukalla had a State coach and was escorted by a body of horsemen in red and white uniforms. The uniform brass buttons had the words 'His Highness Awadh bin Omer al Qu'aiti' on them in Arabic in the centre, in a circle, with the same legend in English around the Arabic script.

TRIBAL GUARD

AL HARAS AL QABALI

From around 1935 British policy in the Protectorates was to encourage State rulers to form their own local armed retinue, or tribal guard, for service within their own territory. Dhala, Haushabi, Audhali and Fadhli Tribal Guards were raised in 1935. The rifles and the ammunition were supplied on loan and remained the property of the Aden Government. By 1940 most of the States had formed their own military units, which were usually officered by friends and relatives of the local ruler. Guards were lightly armed, and in effect constituted a rural constabulary controlled by the local ruler. The term 'tribal guard' usually refers to those forces in the Western Aden Protectorate, but in the Eastern Aden Protectorate the Wahidi Sultanate and Mahra Sultanate also possessed such forces. Tribal guard existed in the States of Alawi Sheikhdom, Amirate of Beihan, Upper Aulaqi Sheikhdom, Upper Aulaqi Sultanate, Lower Aulaqi Sultanate, Audhali Sultanate, Dathina Republic, Amirate of Dhala, Shaib Sheikhdom, Muflahi Sheikhdom, Haushabi Sultanate, Lahej Sultanate, Fadhli Sultanate Armed Police and Lower Yafai Sultanate Armed Police. Upper Yafai Sultanate and Aqrabi Sheikhdom did not possess any disciplined forces of any sort. In 1959 the tribal guard merged with the Government Guards, to form the Federal National Guard of the Federation of Arab Amirates of the South.

UNIFORM

Tribal guard parade dress comprised a khaki shirt, shorts and red *pagri*. Working dress usually consisted of a khaki cloth shirt, and a *footah* (cotton kilt) with khaki *pagri*. Locally made *kuwash* sandals were also worn. Soldiers carried .303 Rifles, SMLE No. 1 Mk III,

and wore a locally made ammunition cartridge belt of leather. The *jambia*, or dagger, was placed in the traditional location at the front of the belt. On 21 May 1937 the governor of Aden authorised the following uniform for senior and junior tribal guard instructors in the Aden Protectorate: Khaki shorts; khaki tunic; khaki shirt, and tie; khaki puttees; dark brown boots; plain buttons; red-on-white cloth shoulder badges APTG (Aden Protectorate Tribal Guard); red sash; red and green *pagri* flash on khaki *pagri*. Badge: a crescent and star. A leather belt was worn over a dark green cummerbund. The uniform was permitted to be worn on official occasions in the colony of Aden, but it had no relation to the Aden Protectorate Levies, or to any of His Majesty's Forces.

WAHIDI TRIBAL GUARD

AL HARAS AL QABALI AL WAHIDI

By about 1886 the British were making treaties with coastal 'rulers' along the South Arabian coastline. Some protection would be afforded to the rulers in return for them attempting to keep the peace along their various stretches of coast, quelling piracy and agreeing not sell their land to anyone else. In the area known as Wahidi there were two separate sultanates – Bir Ali and Balhaf – as well as two apparently independent sheikhdoms of Irqa and Haura Sifla. Treaties were signed with all of them.

In 1951 the sheikhdoms were absorbed into the main Wahidi Sultanate of Balhaf and Azzan, but the Bir Ali Sultanate remained separate until the last Sultan died in 1967. During the early twentieth century a degree of anarchy existed. The Balhaf group of sultans managed to hold on to their area, and with the aid of the Jewish population repelled Aulaqi attempts to take over Habban. By 1939, the 'Peace of Ingrams' began to be established

Tribal Guard at Merta, Western Aden Protectorate, May 1958. The tribesman is dressed in a khaki cloth shirt and *footah*, and locally made sandals. Armed with a SMLE No. 1 Mk III rifle, he carries a locally produced ammunition/cartridge belt and has positioned his *jambia* in its traditional place at the front. His head is covered by a plain Audhali-style headdress. (Major C. Butt)

Airstrip in Wahidi in 1961. This photo was taken following the successful conclusion of a small war with a part of the Qamush tribe, who had thought it their right to raid certain of their neighbours and acquire the goods of travellers without payment. Left to Right; Mulazim Hussain bin Afif, WTG; Ahmed al Mardhoof; the Suleimani Muqaddam; Jim Ellis; Ali Sinna, WTG driver; Bin Said; Rubeiya Ba Sa'a; Ike Dawson, Air Liaison Officer; Residency Mechanic; Mehdi Ba Bakri; navigator of the Twin Pioneer; Ahmed bil Hajri; WTG driver; Mazuq (Nkrumah), Bin Said's driver. Bin Said appears to be carrying an 8mm Mauser. (Jim Ellis)

in Hadhramaut. People were sick and tired of war. A Tribal Guard was raised in Balhaf and comprised 2 officers and 46 men in 1940. Their uniform consisted of khaki shirts and shorts only. The Guard carried out customs and road guard duties in the Balhaf Sultanate and was subsidised by HM Government. The Wahidi Tribal Guard (WTG) were principally recruited from local tribesmen, but also included several Yafa'is, tribesmen from the Qu'aiti area and one or two Jews from Habban. They were regarded as the 'Sultan's men', having played a notable part in the defence of Habban against the Aulaqi.

In 1948, a rabbi of Yemeni origin named Zadok visited Habban and urged the Jewish population to return to the 'Promised Land'. A similar appeal had been made to the Jews of the Yemen. Following negotiations with the Sultan and his advisers the great majority decided to go and travelled to Aden in hired trucks before joining 'Operation Magic Carpet' which would take them to Israel. Unlike the Jews of Yemen they were armed with modern rifles and caused quite a stir when they arrived in Aden 'zamilling' and firing in the air.

In 1957 Major Jock Snell, the Military Assistant in the area, set about retraining the WTG with Hadhrami Bedouin Legion (HBL) assistance, aiming to make it a more effective force. Gradually the Wahidi administration became settled and its military force likewise more experienced and dependable. The populated areas became less turbulent and trouble was confined to the mountains of the south-west corner of the State. With HBL garrisons established in the two main inland settlements of Al Khabr and Mit-haf, the area became relatively stable. This enabled the WTG patrols to penetrate the remotest settlements and grazing areas. Although Wahidi was in the Eastern Aden Protectorate, trade was focused on Aden rather than Mukalla, and when the Federation of

South Arabia was founded the Wahidi decided to become part of the federation. The other Eastern Aden Protectorate States never joined the Federation. Consequently, the WTG became a part of Federal National Guard 2 in 1962. As they were a better trained force in a larger area than any of the other Federated States, they tended to retain a degree of independence. Their commander, Qaid (Major) Mahdi Mohsin Ba Bakri was a Laswadi tribesman from near Habban, and most of the other Wahidi tribes were represented in the force. They protected the security of the State without assistance from Federal National Guard 1.

UNIFORM
The Wahidi Tribal Guard wore khaki shirts, drill shorts and leather belts. Locally made leather equipment was worn on patrol. Headdress consisted of green and white *imama* with black *aqu'al*. After joining the Federal National Guard in 1962 they adopted the dress of that force. The WTG was armed with the .303 Rifle No. 4 Mk I and a few Bren Guns.

ZEYLAH FIELD FORCE
In 1884 an expedition was mounted from Aden to Zeylah (Zeila) on the Somali coast. This field force was raised to relieve the Egyptian garrison of Harrar, a fourteen-day journey inland from the coast by caravan. The garrison was due to return to Egypt and required support in relinquishing its position, as the situation was unstable. According to the *Illustrated London News* of 22 November 1884, the field force sent from Aden consisted of a half-battery of light field artillery (three 7-pdr guns on camels), 150 men of the 4th Bombay Rifles, and a portion of the Aden garrison. The Aden Camel Battery is mentioned by name as a participant.

3

BADGES AND INSIGNIA OF THE POLICE AND ARMED FORCES OF ADEN

1ST YEMEN INFANTRY

1st Yemen Infantry brass shoulder title. (Cliff Lord)

1st Yemen Infantry silver brooch. (Eddie Yates)

ADEN POLICE

Left to right: Headdress badge, with a white metal Tudor Crown, worn until 1954, Aden Police headdress badge, officer's issue, with blue enamel and St Edward's Crown, worn 1954–67, Aden Police headdress badge bearing white metal St Edward's Crown, worn 1954–67. (Cliff Lord)

Aden Police silver collar badge. (Cliff Lord)

Aden Police belt buckle. This heavy base metal buckle was worn on a black leather belt. The Tudor Crown is surmounted by the curved inscription ADEN POLICE. After 1954, the Tudor Crown was replaced by the St Edward's Crown. The officer's number is stamped below the crown. (Cliff Lord)

Aden Police officer's epaulet rank insignia. (Cliff Lord)

Second type of Aden Police collar badge; voided (right) and non-voided (left) styles. (Cliff Lord)

Aden Police officers small shoulder title. White metal. (Cliff Lord)

Aden Police small white metal shoulder title. (Cliff Lord)

Aden Police monogram as worn on fez, 1937. (Cliff Lord)

RAF Regiment Beret Badge, Aden. Limited edition of badges for veterans. On green stiff fabric material. (Cliff Lord)

Aden Police insignia worn on the knob of the pace stick. WW2 and possibly earlier. (Cliff Lord)

ARMY & SOUTH ARABIAN ARMY

APL, FRA & SAA headdress badges and a large APL title. Top row: Bi metal APL badge, APL anodized aluminium badge for British ORs, officer's APL badge. Bottom row: FRA anodized aluminium badge, FRA officer's badge, SAA anodized badge for all ranks. (Cliff Lord)

ADEN PROTECTORATE LEVIES, FEDERAL REGULAR

Unofficial Aden Protectorate Levies cloth shoulder title, green with white lettering. (Cliff Lord)

L to R FRA white metal small shoulder title, FRA anodized aluminium title, SAA anodized shoulder title. Bottom row: APL gilt and silver plate officers collar badge, small APL brass title, FRA and possibly SAA collar badge. The SAA badges were only worn from June to November 1967. (Cliff Lord)

Unofficial locally made APL headdress badge, worn on beret by RAF Regiment personnel during the 1950s. (Cliff Lord)

WO II silver rank badge with green frame and officer's shoulder board star (pip) with green backing. Both anodized aluminium and worn by FRA and SAA. (Cliff Lord)

Officer's APL wire wove headdress badge worn 1957 to 1961. (Cliff Lord)

FRA officer's wire wove headdress badge 1961 to 1967. (David Birtles)

FEDERAL NATIONAL GUARD

Federal National Guard officer's white metal badges. Cap badge, *sedara* badge and probable collar badge or mess dress insignia, worn 1959–1967. Headdress for ORs is brass. Shoulder title in brass or white metal. (Cliff Lord)

Federal National Guard cloth shoulder title green with black embroidery. (Cliff Lord)

GOVERNMENT GUARDS

Government Guard. Officer's bronze headdress badge on left. Crown Agents pattern no. 442, sealed 21 May 1947. Black and brass OR's issue (note, no crown). (Cliff Lord)

Government Guard green *pagri* fringe and black badge. (Eddie Parks)

Government Guards marksman cloth khaki drill patch with black embroidered rifles. (Cliff Lord)

Government Guard cloth shoulder title green with black embroidery. (Cliff Lord)

Government Guard black shoulder title. (Cliff Lord)

Government Guards cloth shoulder title. Khaki drill with black embroidered script. Black script on green felt for officers, black on khaki for other ranks. (Cliff Lord)

TRIBAL GUARD

Tribal insignia:
Top row, left to right: Al Muflahi Sheikhdom; Al Fadli Sultanate; Lower Aulaqi Sultanate. Khaki drill with black script, sealed 10 February 1961.
Middle row, left to right: Al Audali Sultanate; Upper Aulaqi Sheikhdom; Dathina. Khaki drill with black script, sealed 10 February 1961.
Third row, left to right: Ad Dala Emirate; Lower Yafa Sultanate; Beiham Emirate. Khaki drill with black script, sealed 10 February 1961.
Bottom: Al Abdali Sultanate (Abdali being the family name of the Lahej sultans). Khaki drill with black script, sealed 10 February 1961. (Tom Wylie)

HADHRAMI BEDOUIN LEGION

Hadhrami Bedouin Legion chromed headdress badge. (Cliff Lord)

This is a rare example of the first type of headdress badge, seen here affixed to wood, worn by the Hadhrami Bedouin Legion. The inscription reads Bedouin Army in Arabic. (Owain Raw-Reese)

Hadhrami Bedouin Legion white metal shoulder title. The inscription reads Hadhrami Bedouin Army in Arabic. (Cliff Lord)

KATHERI ARMED CONSTABULARY

Katherie Armed Constabulary Brass shoulder title bearing a black inscription of the units' title in Arabic. (Tom Wylie)

MUKALLA REGULAR ARMY

Brass shoulder title worn by the MRA. Die cast by Firmin, London, 1947. Crown Agents Pattern 527. (Tom Wylie)

MUKALLA POLICE AND PRISON

Brass shoulder title produced by Firmin of London. Crown Agents Pattern 708, 1964. (Tom Wylie)

QU'AITI ARMED CONSTABULARY

Qu'aiti Armed Constabulary brass shoulder title worn from 1958 to 1962. Crown Agents pattern 6190 17.3.58. (Tom Wylie)

Qu'aiti Armed Constabulary brass shoulder title 1962. Crown Agents Pattern 9901. (Tom Wylie)

QU'AITI CIVIL POLICE

Qu'aiti Civil Police, al Shurtah al-madaniyyah, brass shoulder title worn by the Mukalla Town Police. (David Birtles)

QU'AITI SULTANATE BAND

Qu'aiti Sultanate Band brass shoulder title. Made by Dowler of Birmingham 1960. Crown Agents Pattern 6998 7.4.60. (Tom Wylie)

LAHEJ POLICE

Lahej Police brass headdress badge. (Cliff Lord)

ADEN RIFLES

Aden Rifles headdress badge (also made without the teardrop frame). (Cliff Lord)

WW2 Air Raid Precautions badge for Aden (unknown unit). (Cliff Lord)

67 Aden Rifles white metal shoulder title. There was a 45 Aden Rifles, but no record found of 67, but has letters of the same time period. (Cliff Lord)

4
AWARDS, ORDERS, DECORATIONS AND MEDALS

AWARDS OF THE ABDALI SULTANATE OF LAHEJ

AWARD OF SULTAN FADHL BIN ALI MOHSIN AL 'ABDALI

This is a circular medallion with possibly a crown suspension, manufactured locally in either Lahej or Aden in gold for Sultan Fadhl. A portrait depicts the Sultan wearing the decoration which appears to have been instituted to coincide with either Queen Victoria's Golden or Diamond Jubilee and the attendant celebrations in Aden in 1887 or 1897 or the visit of the Prince of Wales to Aden at some time during the Sultan's reign. As of writing no further details have been discovered.

LAHEJ 1911 MEDAL

King George V and Queen Mary visited Aden on the way to India and the Dehli Durbar in 1911 is noted in 'The Historical Record of the Imperial Visit to India 1911', that 'a commemorative medallion in honour of the visit to Aden was struck by the Sultan of Lahej'. To date no details of this medallion have been discovered.

ORDER OF THE MORNING STAR

Apparently awarded only once, the Order of the Morning Star represents an interesting tale. In 1910 the Egyptian photographer Riad Shihata visited Lahej to take photographs of the ruler. When the work was completed, Shihata was consulted regarding his reward and told Sultan Ahmad Bin Fadhl Al Abdali that he would accept a decoration. Thus, the Order of the Morning Star was created to meet the photographer's request. Riad Shihata was allowed to design the award and to undertake the manufacture of the badge. As far as is known, the only award was to its initiator, Riad Shihata. The badge is a seven-pointed silver rayed star suspended by a crown, with a central silver medallion, red with a silver dagger point to the left. Around the centre an Arabic inscription 'Ahmad Bin Fadhl Al Abdali Sultan Lahej 1329' (1910 AD). The reverse is plain and the ribbon unknown.

The Order of the Morning Star. (Owain Raw-Rees)

SULTAN AHMED'S BREAST STAR

To date nothing is known of the circumstances of this award. It may be that its manufacture follows the Sultan's return from the Delhi Durbar and was an attempt to institute his own Order. The decoration consists of a gilded silver, hand cast, 24-pointed star, 89mm in diameter. Each alternate ray is set with four clear paste stones. Set horizontally across the upper rays, hilt to the right, is a sabre. The raised central boss of the star is surrounded by a circle of 37 pink paste stones. In the centre a large multi-faceted blue paste stone. This central stone is surrounded by the engraved Arabic inscription, 'Sultan Ahmed Fadhl Sultan Lahej Sultan's Encrusted Sun 1330 Hijjri'. (1330 equates to the Gregorian year 22 December 1911 through to 7 December 1912.) The reverse is plain and bears, left and right, two supporting pins and top and bottom the marks of where a brooch pin was affixed. The details of the ribbon, if any, are unknown. The authors are indebted to Owain Raw-Rees for this information.

Lahej Star. (Owain Raw-Rees)

AWARDS OF THE QU'AITI SULTANATE OF HADHRAMAUT

'Wissam al Imtiaz' – Order of Distinction (Sometimes erroneously referred to in English as the Distinguished Service Medal) – a silver medal with scroll bar suspension.

'Wissam al Khidmat' – Order of Service (Sometimes erroneously referred to in English as the Meritorious Service Medal) – a bronze medal with straight bar suspension.

These medals, instituted on 2 October 1948, were awarded sparingly by Sultan Saleh and his successors, Sultan Awadh and Sultan Ghalib. The obverse consists of an effigy of Saleh bin Ghalib Al Qu'aiti, the Sultan of Shiher and Mukalla, the ruler of Qu'aiti, in ceremonial dress. The reverse is made up of the arms of the Sultan, being the cipher of the Sultan supported by a lion, to the left, and a unicorn. Above which are two crossed sabres, hilts downwards. Below the cipher, on a scroll, is the inscription, in English only, 'H.H. Sultan Sir Saleh bin Ghalib Al Qu`aiti, Sultan of Shiher and Mukalla, K.C.M.G.' At the top of the medal is the Arabic inscription, 'Order of Excellence' or 'Order of Merit'. The medals are 1.42" or 36mm diameter and are of silver and bronze respectively. Suspension is by a scroll bar fixed clamp and a plain bar fixed clamp respectively. The ribbon is 1 ¼" or 31.5mm wide of three equal stripes of red, yellow and blue. If the Orders are bestowed upon military personnel then there is a narrow white central stripe central 2mm wide. These colours echo the national flag – the red being the old Yafa`i colour, the yellow for the desert and the blue for the sea. On the actual flag being a tricolour of these colours on the yellow are three roundels with castles representing the fortified towns of Mukalla, Shihr and Shibam –

Qu'aiti Order of Distinction and the Qu'aiti Order of Service. 'Wissam al Imtiaz' – Order of Distinction (Sometimes erroneously referred to as the Distinguished Service Medal) – a silver medal with scroll bar suspension. 'Wissam al Khidmat' – Order of Service (Sometimes erroneously referred to as the Meritorious Service Medal) – a bronze medal with straight bar suspension. The design of the medals is identical other than the Arabic text on the upper reverse of the medals. The ribbon is the same for both Orders – the Qu'aiti colours of blue, yellow and red – if the Orders were bestowed upon military personnel then there is a narrow white central stripe. (Sultan Ghalib)

the latter on green as it is on land and the former two on blue for the sea because they are ports. The obverse of the medal was designed by Mr Percy Metcalfe – the initials P.M. are visible at the base of the obverse, while the reverse was prepared by the Royal Mint based on image supplied by the Sultanate. The awards were manufactured by The Royal Mint in London. The design of the medals is identical other that the Arabic text on the upper reverse of the medals. Prior to the institution of the DSM and MSM and up to the mid-1950s, the Qu'aiti Sultans had also bestowed the titles of 'Pasha' and 'Beg' in addition to the award of gold swords, *jambias* (daggers) and firearms. (The authors are indebted to H.H. Sultan Ghalib Al Quaiti for his assistance with these awards and Owain Raw-Rees who compiled the details).

ORDER OF HADHRAMAUT
Prior to the Sultan's coronation anniversary, a local goldsmith in Mukalla of Gujerati origin, 'Nattu' was tasked with the manufacture of an example of a proposed Order of Hadhramaut for the Sultan. The design was based on the breast star of the British Order of St. Michael and St. George with the central medallion design replaced with that of the Qu'aiti flag and the Sultan wore it during his coronation ceremonies. The authors are indebted to H.H. Sultan Ghalib Al Quaiti for his assistance with these awards and Owain Raw-Rees who compiled the details.

BRITISH GENERAL SERVICE AND CAMPAIGN SERVICE MEDALS

GENERAL SERVICE MEDAL 1918–1962, WITH CLASP 'ARABIAN PENINSULA'
The GSM with clasp 'Arabian Peninsula' was awarded for service in resisting border raids, and for operations against bands of dissidents in the Arabian Peninsula between 1 January 1957 and 30 June 1960 inclusive. Service of 30 days was required. The medal was authorised by Army Order No. 4 19 January 1923. Six issues of the medal exist. The sixth issue 1953–1964 is described thus:

Obverse: Crowned bust of Queen Elizabeth II and the inscription 'ELIZABETH II DEI GRATIA REGINA F.D.'

Reverse: Winged figure of Victory, standing and placing a wreath on the emblems of the two services. In her left hand is a trident.

> Metal: Silver 36mm diameter.
> Ribbon: 32mm wide purple with a green strip in the centre.
> Suspension: Ornamental swivelling suspender.
> Designer: E. Carter Preston.

The clasp 'Arabian Peninsula' was authorised by Army Order 9, 22 February 1961. A total of 16 clasps for different campaigns were issued. The following local units were entitled to the GSM 1918–62 and the clasp 'Arabian Peninsula':

ADEN PROTECTORATE GOVERNMENT
Aden Protectorate Levies
Government Guards
Hadhrami Bedouin Legion

EASTERN PROTECTORATE
Mukalla Regular Army
Qu'aiti Armed Constabulary
Kathiri Armed Constabulary
Wahidi Tribal Guards

WESTERN PROTECTORATE
For the period 1 January 1957 – 11 February 1959:
Amiri Tribal Guards
Beihan Tribal Guards
Upper Aulaqi Sheikdom Tribal Guards
Aughali Tribal Guards
Fadhli Armed Police
Lower Yafai Armed Police

For the period 1 January 1957 – 11 February 1960:
Lower Aulaqi Sultanate Tribal Guards
Dathina Tribal Guards

For the period 1 January 1957 – 30 June 1960:
Upper Aulaqi Sultanate Tribal Guards
Shu'aibi Tribal Guards
Muflahi Tribal Guards
Haushabi Tribal Guards

For the period 1 April 1959 – 5 October 1959:
Lahej Regular Army
Lahej Tribal Guards

For the period 11 February 1959 – 30 June 1960:
   (Federation of Arab Amirates of the South)
   Federal National Guard

Members of specially approved civilian categories named below who had served with the Forces on land were eligible under the same rules as the Army:
   Navy, Army and Air Force Institutes Staff
   Soldiers', Sailors' and Airmen's Families Association Nursing Service
   British Red Cross Society Welfare Service
   Women's Voluntary Service
   Mission to Mediterranean Garrisons
   Soldiers' and Airmen's Scripture Readers' Association

Members of the following civil category under the jurisdiction of the Aden Protectorate Government were eligible under the same condition as the Army: Civilian employees of the Aden Government, being properly enrolled as Government servants, who were serving with, or in conjunction with, any of the locally raised armed forces.
[Authors' note: The spelling of some State names in this list differs from the map.]

CAMPAIGN SERVICE MEDAL 1962 – WITH CLASP 'RADFAN' AND 'SOUTH ARABIA':

This medal superseded both the Naval General Service Medal 1915 and the 1918 Army and RAF General Service Medal, and was instituted by Ministry of Defence Order No. 61, 6 October 1964.

   Obverse: Crowned bust of Queen Elizabeth II and an inscription 'ELIZABETH II DEI GRATIA REGINA F.D.'
   Reverse: Wreath of oak surrounding the words 'FOR CAMPAIGN SERVICE'.
   Metal: Silver 36mm diameter.
   Ribbon: 32mm wide. Purple with green edges.
   Suspension: Ornamental swivelling suspender.
   Designer: T.H. Paget, OBE

The 'Radfan' clasp was awarded to all British and Federal Forces participating in 14 days continuous service in South Arabia either during the Radfan operation itself, or while operating in a supporting role. The qualifying period was 25 April to 31 July 1964. Authorised by Army Order 36/65.

The 'South Arabia' clasp was awarded for 30 days continuous service in South Arabia, between 1 August 1964 and 30 November 1967. Authorised by Army Order 40/66.

NAVAL GENERAL SERVICE MEDAL 1915–64 WITH CLASP 'ARABIAN PENINSULA'

The medal is silver with the obverse showing the crowned effigy of Queen Elizabeth II, while the reverse bears the image of Britannia on two sea horses travelling through the sea, her left hand resting on the Union Shield and her right holding a trident. The ribbon is white with two narrow red stripes and red edges. The medal was awarded for service in specific operations mounted by the Royal Navy or Royal Marines (unless in Africa or India, for which the appropriate service medal would be awarded). The clasp Arabian Peninsula was awarded for service in operations against dissidents and to counter border raids in the Arabian Peninsula. The qualifying period was 30 days service between 1 January 1957 and 30 June 1960. This included service in or off the Aden Colony or Protectorate, Muscat and Oman and other neighbouring Gulf States.

ORDERS, DECORATIONS AND MEDALS OF THE FEDERATION OF SOUTH ARABIA

It would appear that these orders, decorations and medals were instituted by the Supreme Council in 1963 or early 1964. In all instances the awards were designed by the Permanent Secretary to the Ministry of Defence of the Federation, Colonel J.B. Chaplain DSO, OBE The manufacture was undertaken by Spink and Son of St. James's, London. The following awards, listed in order of precedence, were announced on 16 March 1964:
   Gallantry Medal 1st Class
   The Order of South Arabia 1st Class
   The Order of South Arabia 2nd Class
   The Order of South Arabia 3rd Class
   The Order of South Arabia 4th Class
   Gallantry Medal 2nd Class
   The Order of South Arabia Medal
   Military Service Medal
   Long Service and Good Conduct Medal

Also awarded by the Supreme Council were:
   (a) Supreme Council Commendation to mark acts of bravery performed by any persons which do not entail a gallantry award but nevertheless involve risk to life and merit recognition.

   (b) Certificate of Meritorious Service.

THE ORDER OF SOUTH ARABIA (FEDERATION OF SOUTH ARABIA)

The Order consists of a seven-pointed silver and gilt star with a circular centre depicting an upturned crescent entwined with cloth, between the tips of the crescent a five-pointed star, below which is a sheathed dagger. The reverse is plain. (The medal is of bronze.) Suspension is by a loop through a ring affixed to the uppermost point of the star. The ribbon is 38mm wide in the Federation colours, being of three equal stripes of black, bright green and pale blue, separated by narrow dull yellow stripes. The ribbon of the 4th class is 32mm in diameter, while that of the medal omits the yellow.

The breast star is a seven-pointed rayed silver and gilt star with a central medallion bearing a similar design to the badge surmounted by the inscription 'HERO OF THE ORDER OF SOUTH ARABIA'. Surrounding the central medallion are seven spaced five-pointed stars. The reverse is plain.

This five-class Order with civil and military divisions was awarded for distinguished service to the Federation on the following basis:

Military Division:
   1st Class – 'Hero', officers above the rank of brigadier, or the force commander if only a brigadier

   2nd Class – 'Commander', officers of the rank of brigadier or full colonel

   3rd Class – 'Officer', officers of rank of lieutenant colonel and senior major

Federation of South Arabia, Order of South Arabia First Class Breast Star. (Owain Raw-Rees)

4th Class – 'Member', commissioned officers of the rank of junior major or below

Medal – Soldiers of the rank of warrant officer or below in recognition of specially distinguished or meritorious service

Civil Division:
1st Class – ministers, top-ranking officials and eminent officials for outstanding services

2nd Class – senior officers of the administrative service, heads of professional and technical departments in the civil service, and prominent officials.

3rd Class – officer's substantially holding super-scale posts in the civil service and officials of equivalent status

4th Class – civil service officers of the scale C2 or above (if of under 10 years' service the award is made for outstanding service), and officials of equivalent status

Medal – subordinate grades in the civil service and officials of equivalent status

Size:
1st Class Star 85mm diameter
2nd Class – no details available
3rd Class Badge 44mm diameter
4th Class Badge 44mm diameter
Medal 44mm diameter

The award was manufactured by Spink and Sons Ltd., who between 1965 and 1966 produced the following:
1st Class – 6

2nd Class – 16
3rd Class – 36
4th Class – 72
Medal – 100

The Order is known to have been awarded to the following British personnel:
1st Class – Sir Kennedy Trevaskis, High Commissioner

2nd Class – Brigadier J. Lunt, CBE, Commander FRA & Brigadier G. Viner. Commander FRA

3rd Class – Lt. Col. H.E.R. Watson, MBE, CO 2nd Battalion FRA, Lt. Col. H.J.W. Newton MBE, CO 3rd Battalion FRA & Major J.C.V. Todd, T.D. Training Battalion, FRA

4th Class – Squadron Leader F.X. Grima. Medical Officer, & Squadron Leader R.J.W. Martin. RAF Regiment

Medal – Sgt. R. Goodwins, RAF & Sgt. S. Kelly, REME

Other British personnel were recommended for awards but with the disintegration of the Federation it is uncertain if they were ever presented.

GALLANTRY MEDAL
A two class five-pointed star of gilt and silver respectively. In the centre the badge of the Federation being an upturned crescent entwined with cloth, between the tips of the crescent a five-pointed star, below which is a sheathed dagger. Uppermost is the Arabic inscription 'For Bravery'. Suspension is by a loop affixed to the uppermost point of the stat and on to a horizontal bar bearing four small crescents and stars. The ribbon is bright green. Between 1965 and 1967, Spink and Son Ltd, manufactured twenty-eight 1st Class and forty-eight 2nd Class awards. The medal was awarded for acts of outstanding gallantry by any member of the Federation, whether in combat or at peace. The two classes were as follows:
1st Class – 'Hero' – awarded only for the acts of the most conspicuous bravery in circumstances of extreme danger

2nd Class – 'Companion' – awarded for acts of bravery of a very high order

The award of the medal carried a cash grant of an equivalent of 200 Pounds Sterling for the 1st Class and 100 Pounds Sterling for the 2nd Class.

Federation of South Arabia Gallantry Medal. (Owain Raw-Rees)

MILITARY SERVICE MEDAL

The medal was instituted to replace the British General Service Medal previously awarded to the Federal Forces for military operations in South Arabia. It would appear that this medal was never produced.

LONG SERVICE AND GOOD CONDUCT MEDALS

Federal Regular Army. In the centre two crossed daggers, hilts uppermost which surmount a horizontal scroll. Above the daggers an upturned crescent with a five-pointed star between its tips.

Federal Guard. A crescent with its tips to the right superimposed on which are two crossed rifles, a dagger in between.

Armed Police. A circular wreath with its base at 'seven o'clock' superimposed on which is a truncheon, hilt lowermost.

In all instances the reverse is plain. The medal is 36mm in diameter and of cupro-nickel. Suspension is by a straight bar affixed to the top of the medal. The ribbon is 32mm wide of three equal stripes of black, bright green and scarlet, representing the Federal Guard, Federal Regular Army and the Armed Police. Spink and Son Ltd, manufactured 200 medals in 1965. The medals were awarded to all NCOs of the Federation forces who had successfully completed 15 years of faithful service without serious disciplinary offence. A bar could be awarded on completion of each subsequent period of 5 years. Prior to the incorporation of Aden into the Federation of South Arabia the police were entitled to the Colonial Police Long Service Medal, which had been instituted in 1934. This was awarded to junior officers and below for 18-years full-time and exemplary service. The authors are indebted to Owain Raw-Rees for this information.

APPENDIX I
VOCABULARY USED BY THE SOUTH ARABIAN MILITARY FORCES

The list below consists of words borrowed and sometimes adapted from English, Arabic and the British Indian Army. Most of the words were in use up until at least 1970.

Aqu'al	Camel hobble worn on top of the *kufiya*
Askari/Askar	Armed retainer/retainers
Baghloos	Belt
Box	Kit box or bag
Boot	PT shoe(s)
Burnoos	Blanket
Babu	Clerk (military)
Brenaat	Bren gun
Chaoush	Sergeant from the Turkish rank system
Compodar	Medical Orderly (from compounder of drugs)
Condom	Condemned, effete or useless.
Chaplis	Sandals
Dhobi	Laundryman
Dhobighat	Laundry
Dirsi	Tailor
Drees	Dress/uniform
Deecharge	Discharge (end of service)
Durbeel	Field Glasses
Driwel	Driver (Military Transport)
Durrie	Sleeping mat
Fit	NCO's chevron
Foodah	(gun-) Powder
Footah/Futah	Cotton kilt
Golundauze	A Mughal word, golandaz, which means 'a bringer of roundshot', indicating native artillery
Grade	Trade pay
Habs	Cell/detention
Hakoom	Order/Official arrangement
Hajoom	Attack
Imama	Cloth Arab headdress, sometimes called *Kufiya* or *Shemagh*, introduced by the Arab Legion
Izzat	Status
Jambia	South Arabian curved dagger
Jundi/Junood	Soldier/s
Jundarmarat	Gendarmerie
Jundarma	Gendarme
Jalabot	Small ship (from jollyboat)
Jumhuria	Republic
Kamis	Shirt
Kursh	Medal
Katibah	Battalion
Khulla	Pointed cap around which a *pagri* is wrapped
Kufiya	See *Imama*
Kurta	Indian shirt
Kuwash	Tribal pattern sandals of a type worn from Dahla to the Mushreq
Lainaat	Lines
Lanch	Small-middle sized boat
Ma'ash	Pay

Madfa	Artillery
Makman	Ambush
Manwar	Warship (man o'war)
Mashedda	*Pagri* or Turban
Medalia	Medal ribbon
Moochi	Cobbler
Mumtaz	Blessed/Favoured (congratulatory)
Murbarak	Blessing/Blessed (congratulations)
Murcha	Sangar (dry stone construction)
Na'ib	Governor of a liwa' or province
Nasr	Victory
Nakhauda	Ship's master
Napthatha	Jet aircraft
Pagri	Turban
Punka	Fan/Aircraft propeller
Pantalon	Trousers
Qafilah	Convoy (more civil than military use)
Qa'im	District Commissioner
Qal'ah	fort
Rangroot	Recruit
Rashasha	Machine Gun
Rashun	Rations (common usage for food supplies)
Rhee'aful(at)	Rifle(s)
Rimi	Bullet/Round
Risala	Troop of Cavalry
Sacre	Sugar
Sahib	Sir (pronounced 'saab')
Salaami	Royal/General Salute Parade or special occasion
Sali	Prayers
Sayyid	Saint, also descendant of the Prophet Mohammed (misused as a honorific to flatter an important Arab)
Sedara	Headdress similar to British Army Service Hat (Side Hat) but with the hat badge to the front
Seman	Kit (personal)
Shamla	The loose end protruding above the turban in the manner of a fan
Shanta	Bag
Shay	Tea
Sijon	Prison
Sowar	Cavalry trooper
Switch	Vehicle key (ignition)
Teeb/Tebib	Medicine/Doctor
Tamboor	Tent or vehicle tilt
Taheen	Atta (wheat) flour
Tarboosh	Fez
Top Khana	Artillery (literally 'big gun')
Usra	Cummerbund
Wali	Area Governor
Worsha	Workshops
Yallah	(War cry calling on God 'oh God'). Mostly used in sense of 'let's go', 'get a move on' or 'charge/advance'
Zamil	War song

APPENDIX II
BRITISH AND INDIAN REGIMENTS AND UNITS THAT SERVED IN ADEN

BRITISH BATTALIONS

The system, in which British regular battalions served in Aden before 1914, and after 1919 until 1928, largely conforms to a pattern. (The RAF took responsibility for security from 1928 until 1957). Each year about two battalions left India for Britain after long periods of service in the subcontinent. Generally, one battalion returned directly to the UK, or sometimes via Singapore for a year, and the other relocated to Aden for a year's tour before returning to Britain. The dates are approximate as a regiment would sometimes do part of its 12 months across two separate years. The lists serve only as a guide to the researcher as a fully comprehensive listing was beyond the resources of the writers.

1841	1st Battalion, 6th Foot (half-battalion)
1855	78th Highlanders circa 1855
1858	57th Foot (West Middlesex)
1860–1861	1st Battalion, The King's Own
1862–1865	109th (2nd Leinster)
1866	1st Battalion/2nd Foot (1st Queens)
1868	1st Battalion/7th Foot (1st Royal Fusiliers)
1869	82nd Foot (2nd Lancashire)
1870	3rd Battalion, Rifle Brigade (3RB)
1871	
1872	105th Foot (2nd KOYLI)
1876	55th Foot (2nd Border)
1877	56th Foot (2nd Essex)
1878	1st Battalion/14th Foot (1st West Yorkshire)
1879	1st Battalion/6th Foot (1st Warwickshire)
1880	62nd Foot (became 1st Wiltshire in Aden 1881)
1881	1st Wiltshire
1882	1st Battalion Seaforth Highlanders
1883	1st York & Lancaster
1884	1st Essex
1885	1st South Lancs
1886	2nd Dorset
1887	2nd North Staffords
1888	2nd East Yorks
1889	1st West Riding
1890	2nd Leicestershire
1891	1st Connaught Rangers
1892	2nd King's Liverpool
1893	2nd South Wales Borders
1894	2nd Gloucestershire
1895	2nd West Yorkshire
1896	1st Worcestershire
1897	1st Royal Welsh Fusiliers
1898	2nd Manchester
1898	2nd Notts & Derby
1899	
1900	1st Royal West Kent
1901	1st Royal West Kent
1902–1904	2nd R Dublin Fusiliers

1903–1904	1st Hampshire
1904	1st Buffs
1905	3rd Rifle Brigade
1906	2nd KOSB
1907	2nd Suffolk
1908	1st Bedfordshire
1908	1st Queens
1910–1911	1st Northamptonshire
1910	1st Lincolnshire
1911	1st Warwickshire
1912	1st Middlesex
1913	1st Royal Irish Fusiliers
1914	1st Lancashire Fusiliers
1915	1st/4th Buffs and 1st/1st Brecknock (South Wales Borderers)
1916	1th/4th Duke of Cornwall's Light Infantry
1917	1th/6th East Surry Regt
1918	1st/7th Hampshire Regt
1919	1st Kings Shropshire Light Infantry
1920	2nd Royal Fusiliers
1921	
1922	2nd Buffs
1923	
1924	1st Border
1925	1st Royal Scots
1926	2nd Devonshire
1927	2nd South Wales Borderers
1928	1st Welch

(See separate list for WW2)

ROYAL GARRISON ARTILLERY

In the 15 years or so before the First World War it was customary to rotate 2 or 3 companies of the RGA from India and back to India every two years. This pattern was modified when 76 Company RGA stayed on from 1906 until 1920 and was joined by 61 Company RGA in 1914–1920. There appears to be no RGA presence 1920–1924. 7 Heavy Battery RA was stationed in Aden from June 1924 until July 1927.

1900–1902	8 Eastern, 18 Southern, 16 Western Company, RGA
1902–1904	45, 54, 55 Company, RGA
1904–1906	51, 60, 70 Company, RGA
1906–1908	69, 76 Company, RGA
1908–1910	76 Company, RGA
1910–1912	64, 76 Company, RGA
1912–1914	62, 70, 76 Company, RGA
1914–1920	61, 76 Company, RGA
1924–1927	7 Heavy Battery, RA

POST-SECOND WORLD WAR ARMY UNITS IN ADEN
Artillery
5th Battery, 14 Field Regiment (October 1958–October 1959)
1 Battery, 14 Field Regiment (October 1959–September 1960)
C Troop, 97 Battery 33 Para Field Regiment (April 1958)
C Battery, RHA (September 1960–January 1962)
J Battery, RHA (January 1962–August 1962)
D Battery, RHA (August 1962–February 1963)
C Battery, RHA (February 1963–July 1963)
J Battery, RHA (July 1963–January 1964)
D Battery, RHA (January 1964–October 1964)

J Battery, RHA (18 March 1964–1 May 1964)
45 Field Regiment (April 1964–July 1964)
20 Commando Amphibious Observation Battery (5 May 1964–31 December 1964)
67 Field Battery (8 May 1964–29 June 1964)
28 Medium Battery (9 May 1964–19 June 1964)
25 Field Battery (9 May 1964–19 June 1964)
170 Imjin Battery, 7th Regiment, RHA (one troop) (1964)
25 Light Battery (19 June 1964–1 September 1965)
67 Light Battery (29 June 1964–1 September 1965)
19 Light Regiment (August 1964–August 1965)
F Para Battery, RHA (1 May 1965–15 October 1965)
E Battery, RHA (1 September 1965–1 June 1967)
B Battery, RHA (1 September 1965–1 June 1967)
A Battery, RHA (1 September 1965–1 June 1967)
1 Light Regiment, RHA (18 September 1965–20 April 1966)
1 Regiment, RHA (20 April 1966–20 June 1967)
28 Light Battery (1 January 1965–10 September 1965)
G Para Battery, RHA (1 April 1965–1 May 1965)
4 Light Battery (1 April 1967–1 July 1967)
3 Light Battery (1 May 1967–1 September 1967)
31 Light Battery (1 June 1967–1 November 1967)
8 Commando Light Battery (1 October 1967–1 November 1967)
8 Commando Light Battery (1 November 1967–1 February 1968)
47 Light Regiment (June–August 1967)

Engineers
2 Field Survey Depot (1963–1966)
3 Field Squadron, RE (1963–1967)
6 Field Park Squadron (1964–1965)
9 (Para) Field Squadron, RE (1964–1965)
10 Airfield Squadron, RE (1965–1967)
12 Field Squadron, RE (1963–1964)
13 Field Survey Squadron (1963–1966)
15 Field Park Squadron (1963–1964)
19 Topographical Squadron (1963–1966)
20 Field Squadron (1965–1966)
24 Field Squadron, RE (1964–1965)
30 Field Squadron, RE (1966–1967)
32 Field Squadron (1963)
34 Field Squadron, RE (1 troop)
39 Field Squadron, RE (1967)
48 Field Squadron, RE (1963–1964)
A Troop 50 Field Squadron, RE (September 1967–November 1967)
60 Field Squadron, RE (1964–1965)
63 Field Park Squadron, RE (1964–1967)
73 Field Squadron, RE (1965)
261 Postal Unit, RE
300 Field Squadron, RE
131 Para Engineer Regiment, TA (1965)
513 Specialist Team, RE
516 Petrol Oil Lubricants (POL) (1964–1965)
521 STRE Well Drilling (1964–1965)
523 STRE Works Agency

Signals
Aden Signal Section (1927–?)
Aden Command Signal Troop (?-1949)
65 Wing Troop, 4 Air Formation Signals (1949–?)
HQ British Forces Arabian Peninsula (Independent) Signal Squadron (1958–1959/1960)

222 (Air Formation) Signal Squadron (1959/1960–1967)

39 Infantry Brigade Signal Squadron (213 Signal Sqn) (1964)

24 Infantry Brigade Signal Squadron (210 Signal Sqn) (1964–1967)

254 Signal Squadron (Absorbed into 15 Signal Regt) (1959/1960–1965)

603 (Mideast) Signal Troop absorbed into 15 Signal Regiment (1965)

643 (Comms Security) Signal Troop (formed in Aden in 1964). Absorbed into 15 Signal Regiment 1965

15 Signal Regiment (1965–1967)

Armour

Sqn, Life Guards (July 1955–April 1956)

Sqn, 15th/19th The King's Royal Hussars (April 1956–November 1957)

B Sqn, 13th/18th Hussars (October 1957–September 58)

Sqn, Life Guards (September 1958–November 1959)

1st The Royal Dragoons (November 1959–December 1960)

C Sqn, Queen's Own Hussars (February 1960–December 1960)

C Sqn, 3rd Carabiniers (November 1960–November 1961)

11th Hussars (November 1960–November 1961)

17th/21st Lancers (HQ, A Sqn & B Sqn rotating from Persian Gulf October 1961–October 1962)

Queens Royal Irish Hussars (November 1961–November 1962)

9th/12th Royal Lancers (September 1962–July 1963)

Royal Scots Greys (HQ, A Sqn & B Sqn rotating from Persian Gulf October 1962–November 1963)

D Sqn, 4 Royal Tank Regiment (August 1963–August 1964)

16th/5th Queen's Royal Lancers (November 1963–December 1964)

10th Royal Hussars (August 1964–August 1965)

5th Royal Inniskilling Dragoon Guards (HQ, A Sqn & B Sqn rotating from Persian Gulf December 1964–December 1965)

4th/7th Royal Dragoon Guards (August 1965–September 1966)

1 Royal Tank Regiment (December 1965–1967)

1st Queen's Dragoon Guards (September 1966–July 1967)

Queen's Own Hussars (July 1967–October 1967)

C Sqn 13th/18th Hussars (March 1967–May 1967)

Infantry

1st Battalion, Seaforth Highlanders (July 1955–October 1955)

1st Battalion, King's Own Yorkshire Light Infantry (October 1955–April 1956)

1st Battalion, Durham Light Infantry (November 1956–February 1957)

1st Battalion, Gloucestershire Regiment (April 1956–September 1956)

1st Battalion, Queen's Own Cameron Highlanders (September 1956–March 1958)

1st Battalion, Prince of Wales's Own Regiment of Yorkshire (September 1958–June 1959)

1st Battalion, King's Shropshire Light Infantry (1958, two Companies)

1st Battalion, York & Lancaster Regiment (1958)

1st Battalion, The Buffs (March 1958–January 1959)

1st Battalion, Royal Lincolnshire Regiment (July 1958–September 1958)

1st Battalion, Royal Warwickshire Regiment (August 1959–April 1960)

1st Battalion, Northamptonshire Regiment (January 1959–January 1960)

1st Battalion, Royal Highland Fusiliers (January 1960–January 1961)

1st Battalion, Queen's Royal Surry Regiment (January 1961–February 1962)

1st Battalion, King's Own Scottish Borderers (February 1962–February 1964)

1st Battalion, East Anglian Regiment (February 1964–September 1965), retitled 1st Royal Anglian (December 1964)

1st Battalion, King's Own Scottish Borderers (April 1964–July 1964)

B and C Company, 3rd Battalion, Parachute Regiment (April 1964–July 1964)

A Sqn, 22 Special Air Service (April 1964–1966)

3rd Battalion, Parachute Regiment (June 1964–February 1965)

2nd Battalion, Coldstream Guards (October 1964–October 1965)

1st Battalion, Royal Scots (May 1964–February 1965)

1st Battalion, Royal Sussex Regiment (April 1965–October 1965)

4th Battalion, Royal Anglian Regiment (February 1965–August 1965)

1st Battalion, King's Own Yorkshire Light Infantry (August 1965–May 1966)

1st Battalion, Prince of Wales's Own Regiment of Yorkshire (September 1965–Sept 1966).

1st Battalion, Welsh Guards (October 1965–October 1966)

1st Battalion, Coldstream Guards (October 1965–April 1966)

B Company, 1st Battalion, Gloucestershire Regiment (December 1965–1966)

1st Battalion, Somerset and Cornwall Light Infantry (April 1966–October 1966)

1st Battalion, Loyal Regiment (One Company rotating every 2 months July 1966–January 1967)

3rd Battalion, Royal Anglian Regiment (October 1966–May 1967)

1st Battalion, Cameronians (May 1966–February 1967)

One Company, 1st Battalion, Royal Irish Fusiliers (1966)

1st Battalion, Royal Northumberland Fusiliers (September 1966–June 1967)

1st Battalion, Irish Guards (October 1966–August 1967)

1st Battalion, Lancashire Regiment (February 1967–August 1967)

C Company, 1st Battalion, King's Own Royal Border Regiment (February 1967–November 1967)

B Sqn, 5 RTR (April 1967–July 1967)

1st Battalion, Parachute Regiment (May 1967–November 1967)

1st Battalion, Prince of Wales's Own Regiment of Yorkshire (June 1967–November 1967)

1st Battalion, South Wales Borderers (January 1967–November 1967)

1st Battalion, Argyll and Sutherland Highlanders (June 1967–November 1967)

Royal Marines

45 Commando, RM (April 1960–August 1967)

42 Commando, RM (11th October 1967–November 1967)

Royal Army Service Corps (to 1965)

2 Company (General Transport), RASC

16 Company (Air Despatch), RASC, A Air Supply Platoon detached to Aden 1961)

60 Company (24 Brigade) RASC, 1964

76 Company RASC, 1960

90 Company (Motor Transport) RASC (raised 1 December 1957)
HQ Company
142 Supply Platoon

Royal Corps of Transport (from 1965)
1 Sqn RCT
2 Sqn RCT
7 Sqn RCT (one platoon)
16 Air Despatch Sqn, RCT
51 Port Sqn, RCT
57 Port Sqn, RCT
60 Sqn, RCT
Joint Services Port Unit
LCT (Army) Sqn, RCT

Royal Pioneer Corps
518 Company, RPC

Army Air Corps.
653 Squadron AAC – later 3 Wing AAC
   8 Flight
   15 Flight
   16 Flight

Royal Army Ordnance Corps
Ordnance Depot Aden
Stats and Records Office RAOC, Fort Morbut 1966–1967
Ammunition Depot Khormaksar, RAOC, Singapore Lines
16 Para Heavy Drop Company, RAOC
24 Ordnance Field Park, RAOC, Falaise

Royal Army Medical Corps
24 (Airportable) Field Ambulance, RAMC

Royal Military Police
Port Security Force, RMP
24 Brigade Provost Unit, RMP

Royal Army Pay Corps
518 Company, RPC

Royal Electrical and Mechanical Engineers
52 Command Workshop Aden Garrison
1 Infantry Workshop REME, absorbed 13 Armoured Workshop by 1964
22 Eng Equip Workshop, REME

Intelligence Corps
15 Int Platoon

Women's Royal Army Corps
28 Independent Company WRAC

RAF Regiment
See RAF section for list of squadrons

Indian Battalions
1882–1883   22nd Bombay Infantry
1884–1885   4th Bombay Rifles
1886–1887   9th Bombay Infantry
1888–1889   3rd Bombay Light Infantry

1890–1891   17th Bombay Infantry
1892–1893   16th Bombay Infantry
1894–1896   13th Bombay Infantry
1896–1900   10th Bombay Light Infantry
1900   5th Bombay Infantry
1901   1st Grenadier Bombay Infantry
1902   1th Grenadier Bombay Infantry (renamed 101st Bombay Grenadiers in 1903)
1903–1904   101st Bombay Grenadiers
1903–1904   102nd Bombay Grenadiers
1904–1905   94th Russell's Infantry
1904 123   Outram's Rifles
1905 102   Bombay Grenadiers
1906–1907   116th Mahrattas
1906–1907   81th Pioneers
1908–1909   113th Infantry
1909–1912   108th Infantry
1912–1913   18th Infantry
1914   109th Infantry
1914–1915   23rd Sikh Pioneers
1915–1916   108th Infantry
1916   108th Infantry
1916   5th Carnatic Infantry
1916   69th Punjabis
1916   129th Duke of Connaught's Own
1916–1917   33rd Punjabis
1916–1918   75th Carnatic Infantry
1917   109th Infantry
1917   Malay States Guides
1918   69th Punjabis
1918–1919   1st/7th Duke of Connaught's Own Rajputs
1919   1st Brahmans
1925–1926   5th/12th Frontier Force
1926–1928   4th/11th Sikhs
1927–   5th/10th Baluchs

The authors are indebted to Todd Mills, Frank Stevens and Graeme Watson for much of the order-of-battle information.

APPENDIX III
TABLE 17: BRITISH RESIDENTS AND POLITICAL AGENTS AT ADEN

British Residents at Aden
Political Agents

Captain S.B. Haines, Indian Navy	1839–1854
Major General J. Outram	1854–1856
Political Residents	
Colonel W.M. Coghlan	1856–1862
Major General R.W. Honner	1862
Colonel W.M. Coghlan	1862–1863
Major W.L. Merewether	1863–1867
Major General Sir E.L. Russell	1867–1870
Major General C.W. Tremenheere	1870–1872
Brigadier General J.W. Schneider	1872–1877
Brigadier General F.A.E. Loch	1877–1882
Brigadier General J. Blair	1882–1885
Brigadier General A.G.F. Hogg	1885–1890
Brigadier General J. Jopp	1890–1895
Brigadier General C.A. Cunningham	1895–1899
Brigadier General G. O'Moore Creagh	1899–1901
Brigadier General P.J. Maitland	1901–1904
Major General H.M. Mason	1904–1906
Major General E. de Brath	1906–1910
Brigadier General J.A. Bell	1910–1914
Brigadier General C.H.U. Price	1915
Major General J.M. Stewart	1916–1920
Major General T.E. Scott	1920–1925
Major General J.H.K. Stewart	1925–1928
Lieutenant Colonel G.S. Symes	1928–1930
Lieutenant Colonel B.R. Reilly	1930–1932
Chief Commissioner	
Lieutenant Colonel B.R. Reilly	1932–1937
Governors	
Sir B.R. Reilly	1937–1940
Sir J.H. Hall	1940–1944
Sir R. Champion	1944–1951
Sir T. Hickinbotham	1951–1956
Sir W. Luce	1956–1960
Sir C.H. Johnston	1960–1963
High Commissioners	
Sir K Trevaskis	1963–1965
Sir R. Turnbull	1965–1967
Sir Humphrey Trevelyan	1967

BIBLIOGRAPHY

PRIMARY SOURCES – UNPUBLISHED
Authors' Archives
Anon. 'A' Flight No. 10 Armoured Car Squadron. Aden Protectorate Levies. Diary of events commencing 29th August 1956.
Anon. Aden 1958–61. n.d.
Anon. 'Arabian Journey', Unpublished article, n.d.
Anon. 'OP Outpost, Report on Ops by 3 APL 24 Apr – 27 May 60', Restricted, 3 APL Dhala, G/3/4, Aug 60.
Anon. RAF Regiment and Associated Forces in Aden. n.d.
Anon. South Arabian Military Forces. n.d.
Chaplain to the FRA 'Aden', Untitled articles, n.d.
Butt, C.R. 'APL Reminiscence and Notes', unpublished assorted notes and documents, 1992–98.
Butt, C.R. Merta Road Incident June 1958.
Ellis, J. 'Unit Histories of the EAP, As Recalled by Jim Ellis', unpublished assorted documents, 1986–99
Moloney, R.J. Untitled article on West Aden Protectorate, November 3, 1962.
Thomas, C.B., D.S.O., M.C., Major General Sandy, History of 4 FRA. n.d.
Tudor Pole, C.G. Short History of the Aden Protectorate Levies. (April 1928 – March 1944). n.d.

British Library, India Office Library and Records, London
R/20/A/164, Aden Irregular Horse.
R/20/B/180, Senior and Junior Tribal Guard Instructors Uniform Authorisation 1937.
R/20/B/180, Tribal Guards Instructors.
R/20/B/182, Dress Regulations for Gazetted Officers of the Aden Police, based on Colonial Police Service dress regulations for Gazetted Ranks, May 1938.
R/20/B/296, Letter from Commissioner of Police, Aden, to Legal Adviser, Aden, 3 August 1940.
R/20/B/1206, Extract from the minutes of a meeting held at the Secretariat regarding the duties of the Government Guards, 1938.
R/20/C/810 Sealed Patterns from the Crown Agents.
R/20/C/1008 Mukalla Artillery.
R/20/C/1391 Armed Forces in the Hadhramaut, Report by Mr. Sheppard.
R/20/G/318, Police and Police Arrangements, pp.17–19.
P/765 293/40 Letter from Resident Adviser Mukalla.
C/3802 REF Aden 5028/2/AD Lahej Trained Forces.
Legal Supplement No2 Aden Colony Gazette No. 44 19 September 1946 Government Guard Ordinance 1943.
No. 26/1/54 New Flash for Uniform Government Guard.
GG/1/1/131 Tribal Guard Instructors ranks in Government Guard.

Directorate of Land Service Ammunition, Didcot
Starling, Major J.A. Unit Diary 1401 (Aden) Company.
Starling, Major J.A. Unit Diary 1402 (Aden) Company.
Starling, Major J.A. Unit Diary 1422 (Sultan Saleh's Hadramaut) Company.

MOD (RAF) Historical Section, London
Anon. RAF Regiment and Associated Forces in Aden. n.d.
APL/S.2/7.Air, Appendix 'B' to 540, 'Report on an Escort to the Government Guard Nisab-Robat-Nisab. 15th June 1955', Background Information.

National Army Museum, London
54/Misc/6552, 'APL, FRA, Insignia'
Public Relations and Information Department, Aden, 'Operations Begin Against Dissidents in Western Aden Protectorate', Press Communiqué No. 255/55, 10 July, 1955.

The War Office
'Grant of the General Service Medal for Service in the Arabian Peninsula', Special Army Orders No. 9, 22nd February 1961. 68/General/9562 A.O. 9/1961.

PRIMARY SOURCES – PUBLISHED
Colonial Reports Annual 1937.
Colonial Reports Annual 1938.
'Composition of the Indian Expeditionary Forces', 01 February 1918 to 15 November 1919.
'Detail of Indian Units Serving out of India', 15 February 1920 to 01 May 1921.
Indian Army List, 1920 (for 45th Aden Rifles see pp.860).
The Inaugural Ceremony For The Federal Union Of The Amirates of Baihan And Dhala' And the Sultanates of 'Audhali And Fadhli And Yafa'i And The 'Upper' Aulaqi Shaikhdom As The Federation Of Arab Amirates Of The South. Programme. Aden: Government Printer, 11 February 1959.
'Military Report on the Aden Protectorate', Simla: General Staff, 1915.
Port of Aden Annual 1953–54 (for Government Guards see pp.19–21).
'Report by GOC, Aden, On the Operations of the Aden Field Force, 1st April – 18th August 1917', Simla: General Staff, 1917.
'Report by Major General Sir G.J. Younghusband, K C.I.E., C.B., on the Action at Shaikh 'Othman 21st July 1915', Simla: General Staff, 1915.
'Summary of the Administration of Lord Curzon of Kedleston, Viceroy and Governor-General of India, in the Military Department, I. January 1899–April 1904. II. December 1904–November 1905' Simla: Government Central Branch Press, 1906.

SECONDARY SOURCES

Newspaper Articles and Magazines
Anon. 'Aden. A Horrible Little War', FlyPast, October 1998, pp.116–120.
Anon. Letter on Berbera Landings, in The Royal Pioneer, No. 125, December 1975, pp.31–32.
Anon. 'The New Desert Rats Guard Troubled Aden', Illustrated, July 7, 1956, pp.9–13.
Anon. 'Warning by Fire in Murder Valley', Illustrated, July 14, 1956, pp.23–25.
Ash, T. 'Island Without Dogs', The Wire Magazine, June–July 1965, pp.170–173.
Cambridgeshire Weekly News, Thursday, November 7, 1985, pp.21. Article on Berbera Landings.

Eilts, H.F. 'Along the Incense Roads of Aden', National Geographic Magazine, Vol. CXI, no. 2, February 1957.
Hutchinson, A.M.C. 'The Hadrami Bedouin Legion', Royal East Asiatic Society Magazine, date unknown.
Joy, G.A. A Summary of the Raising and Training of the 1st Yemen Infantry and its Possibilities and Political Significance in South-West Arabia, Journal of the Central Asian Society VOL. X1. 1924 Part II.
Lunt, James 'Evolution of an Army', Journal of the Royal United Services Institute, parts 1 and 2, 1965.
Mullis, T.R. Maj. 'The Limits of Air Control: The RAF Experience in Aden, 1926–1967', Research paper presented to the Air Command and Staff College, March 1997.
Peter Taylor, Unforgettable Years, FlyPast, July 2001, pp.60–68.
Raw-Rees O. 'The Awards of the Federation of South Arabia', The Miscellany of Honours, No.11, 1997, published by The Orders and Medals Research Society.
Raw-Rees O. 'The Awards of the Sultanate of Lahej', The Medal Collector, The Journal of the Orders and Medals Society of America, Vol.47, no. 8, October 1996.

Books
Allfree, P.S., Hawks of the Hadhramaut (London: Robert Hale Ltd, 1967)
Anon, The Historical Record of the Imperial Visit to India 1911 (London: John Murray, 1914)
Anon, The History of the Corps of Royal Engineers Volume X (1946–1960) (Chatham: Institution of Royal Engineers, 1986)
Anon, The History of the Corps of Royal Engineers Volume XI (1960–1980) (Chatham: Institution of Royal Engineers, 1993)
Anon, The Punjab and the War (Lahore: Suptdt. Govt. Printing, 1922)
Barr, James, Lords of the Desert: Britain's Struggle with America to Dominate the Middle East (London: Simon & Schuster UK Ltd, 2018)
Becke, A.F., History of the Great War, Order of Battle Part 4 (London: H.M. Stationery Office, 1945)
Belhaven and Stenton, Lord, The Uneven Road (London, 1966)
Bousted, Hugh, The Wind of Morning (London: Chatto and Windus, 1971)
Corbally, Lt. Col. M.J.P.M., The Royal Ulster Rifles 1793–1960 (Arbroath, 1960)
Corps of Signals Committee, History of the Corps of Signals Volume I (New Delhi: Corps of Signals Committee, Signals Directorate, A.H.Q., 1975)
Crouch, Michael, An Element of Luck (The Radcliffe Press, London, 1993)
Cunliffe, M, The Royal Irish Fusiliers 1793–1968 (Oxford: Oxford University Press, 1970)
Drew, Lt. H.T.B., The War Effort of New Zealand (Auckland: Whitcombe and Tombs, 1923)
Edwards, Frank, The Gaysh: A History of the Aden Protectorate Levies 1927–61 and the Federal Regular Army of South Arabia 1961–1967 (Helion & Company Ltd, Solihull, 2004)
Gavin, R.J. Aden Under British Rule 1839–1967 (London: C. Hurst and Co, 1975)
Graham, Brig. Gen. C.A.L., The History of the Indian Mountain Artillery (Aldershot: Gale and Polden, 1957)
Harper, S. Last Sunset, What Happened in Aden (London: Collins, 1978)

Hickinbotham, Tom, *Aden* (London: Constable and Company, 1958)

Ingrams, Harold, *Arabia and the Isles* (London: John Murray, 1966)

Johnston, Charles, *The View From Steamer Point* (London: Collins, 1964)

Joslin, E.C., A.R. Litherland and B.T. Simpkin, *British Battles and Medals* (London: Spink, 1988)

Kimbell, Alex. *Think Like a Bird, An Army Pilots Story* (Airlife Publishing Ltd. Shrewsbury, 2000)

Ledger, David, *Shifting Sands* (London: Peninsular Publishing, 1983)

Lee, Air Chief Marshal Sir David, *Flight from the Middle East* (London: HMSO, 1980)

Little, Tom, *South Arabia* (London: Pall Mall Press, 1986)

Lord, Cliff and Watson Graham, *The Royal Corps of Signals: Unit Histories of the Corps (1920–2001) and its Antecedents* (Solihull: Helion, 2003)

Lucas, Sir Charles, *The Empire at War, Volume V* (Oxford: Oxford University Press, 1926)

Lunt, James, *Imperial Sunset, Frontier Soldiering in the 20th Century* (London: Macdonald, 1981)

Lunt, James, *The Barren Rocks of Aden* (London: Herbert Jenkins Ltd. 1966)

Macmunn, Lieut. Gen. Sir G, *Military Operations Egypt and Palestine, From the Outbreak of War with Germany to June 1917* (London: HM Stationery Office, 1928)

Mehra, Major General K.C., *A History of the Army Ordnance Corps 1775–1974* (AOC Directorate, 1980)

Nevins, E.M., *Forces of the British Empire 1914* (Vandamere Press, Virginia, 1992)

Nicolle, D., *Lawrence and the Arab Revolts* (London: Osprey, 1989)

Oliver, Kingsley M., *Through Adversity: The History of the Royal Air Force Regiment* (Rushden: Forces & Corporate Publishing Ltd, 1997)

Omissi, D.E., *Air Power and Colonial Control (The RAF 1919–1939)* (Manchester: Manchester University Press, 1990)

Paget, Julian. *Last Post: Aden 1964–1967* (Plymouth: Faber and Faber, 1969)

Peter Hinchcliffe, John T. Ducker & Maria Holt, *Without Glory in Arabia: The British Retreat from Aden* (London: I.B.Tauris and Co Ltd, 2006)

Philby, J.B. *Sheba's Daughters, Being a Record of Travel in Southern Arabia* (London: Methuen & Co., 1939)

Rathbone Low, C., *History of The Indian Navy, Volume II* (Calcutta, 1877)

Reed, Stanley, *The King and Queen in India* (Bombay: Benneti, Coleman and Co., 1912)

Romer, Major C.F., and A.E. Mainwaring, *The Second Battalion Royal Dublin Fusiliers in the South African War With a Description of the Operations in the Aden Hinterland* (London: A.L. Humphreys, 1908)

Sandes, Lt. Col. E.W.C., *The Indian Sappers and Miners* (Chatham: Institution of Royal Engineers, 1948)

Singh, Inder, *History of the Malay States Guides, 1873–1919* (Penang: Cathay Printers, 1965)

Thomas, W.B., *Pathways to Adventure, An Extraordinary Life* (Hororata: Dryden Press, 2004)

Trevaskis, Sir Kennedy, *Shades of Amber* (London: Hutchinson, 1968)

Van Der Bijl, Nick, *British Military Operations in Aden & Radfan: 100 Years of British Colonial Rule* (Barnsley: Pen and Sword Books Ltd, 2014)

Walker, Jonathan, *Aden Insurgency; The Savage War in South Arabia 1962–1967* (Staplehurst: Spellmount, 2005)

ABOUT THE AUTHORS

Cliff Lord served in Britain's Royal Signals during the 1960s as a cipher operator in England, Germany and on active service in Aden and the East Aden Protectorate. Following his military service, Cliff worked in Paris for the Washington Post and later moved to New Zealand working as a computer operator, a communications network controller for Air New Zealand and Team Leader International Operations for the Southern Cross fibre optics trans pacific cable before retiring. He is Honorary Historian for Royal New Zealand Corps of Signals. Cliff has written twelve books, including this one, on military history including SIGINT, and insignia, and this is his third instalment for Helion's @War series.

The late David Birtles died before the second edition came out. David was a keen collector of Aden badges and Aden History. He served for a few years in the Merchant Navy before joining Royal Signals. He was posted to Aden in 1960 and spent a period of time serving with the Aden Protectorate Levies. After leaving the army he became active in security and owned his own company. He was also involved in driving and motorcycle instruction, in addition to police dog training and handler instruction.